P9-CBK-348

Home Improvement Tools & Equipment

David H. Jacobs, Jr.

TECHNICAL COLLEGE OF THE LOWCOUNTRY
LEARNING RESOURCES CENTER
POST OFFICE BOX 1288
BEAUFORT, SOUTH CAROLINA 29901-1288

TAB Books
Division of McGraw-Hill, Inc.
Blue Ridge Summit, PA 17294-0850

TECHNICAL COLLEGE OF THE LOWCOUNTRY
LEARNING RESOURCES CENTER
POST OFFICE BOX 1288
BEAUFORT, SOUTH CAROLINA 29901-1288

Disclaimer

The home-improvement designs and views expressed by the author are not necessarily approved by Makita USA, Inc. Makita USA, Inc., shall not be held liable in any way for any action arising from the contents of this book, including, but not limited to, damages or bodily injury caused in whole or in part, by the recommendations or advice contained herein.

FIRST EDITION
FIRST PRINTING

©1994 by **TAB Books**.
TAB Books is a division of McGraw-Hill, Inc.

Printed in the United States of America. All rights reserved. The publisher takes no responsibility for the use of any of the materials or methods described in this book, nor for the products thereof.

Library of Congress Cataloging-in-Publication Data

Jacobs, David H.
   Home improvement tools & equipment / by David H. Jacobs, Jr.
     p.   cm.
   Includes index.
   ISBN 0-8306-4420-2 (pbk.)
     1. Dwellings—Remodeling—Equipment and supplies.   I. Title.
   II. Title: Home improvement tools and equipment.
   TH4816.J35 1993
   643'.7—dc20   93-28711
                                                         CIP

Acquisitions editor: Kimberly Tabor
Editorial team: Robert Burdette, Editor
               Susan Wahlman, Managing Editor
               Joanne Slike, Executive Editor
               Stacey Spurlock, Indexer
Production team: Katherine G. Brown, Director
               Tina M. Sourbier, Coding
               Rose McFarland, Layout
               Joan Wieland, Proofreading
Design team: Jaclyn J. Boone, Designer
            Brian Allison, Associate Designer
Cover design: Graphics Plus, Hanover, Pa.   4402
Cover photograph: Eden Arts, Seattle, Wa.   HT1

CONTENTS

Acknowledgments

Although many home-improvement projects can be accomplished by one person, lots of tasks require help from others. Writing a book about home-improvement tools and equipment is no different, and I would like to thank a number of special people for their assistance and support throughout this endeavor.

Jack Hori is senior vice president and Roy Thompson is the product marketing manager for Makita U.S.A., Inc. Their efforts in providing me with answers to questions, technical information, and product samples were exceptional.

For tape measurers, hand tools, hardware, and tools for finishing concrete and drywall, I sought the assistance of Francis Hummel, director of marketing for The Stanley Works. He has been most supportive in providing products used for do-it-yourself projects and photo sessions.

Hilarie Meyer, associate merchandising manager for Campbell Hausfeld, was responsible for the compressed-air systems presented in this book. Campbell Hausfeld manufactures a number of air compressors and various pneumatic tools and accessories designed for the needs of do-it-yourself homeowners and professional tradespeople.

To help complete tool and equipment needs for projects and photo sessions, I was fortunate to gain the support of David Martel, marketing manager for Central Purchasing, Inc. (Harbor Freight Tools).

Along with tools and equipment, every home-improvement project requires building materials. Rob Guzikowski, marketing manager for the Simpson Strong-Tie Company, Inc., came through with numerous strong-tie connectors and technical information about the hundreds of connectors available.

Updating older homes almost always includes installing new windows that feature excellent insulating characteristics and beautiful designs. I want to thank Tom Tracy, advertising manager, and Ron Reinhardt, customer service representative, from Eagle Windows and Doors for their support in providing windows and technical assistance.

For information on wood and wood products, I was overwhelmed by the material sent by Timm Locke, manager product publicity for the Western Wood Products Association; Maryann Olson, project coordinator/public relations for the American Plywood Association; and Don Meucci, media relations and marketing director for the Cedar Shake and Shingle Bureau.

My sincere gratitude is extended to the following people and the companies they represent: Sureka Reddy, associate product manager for Autodesk Retail Products; Betty Talley, manager marketing services for the American Tool Companies; Patricia McGirr, marketing manager for Alta Industries; Dana Young, vice president of marketing for PanelLift Telpro, Inc.; Dick Warden, general manager for Structron Corporation; Dave Shanahan, director of marketing for Keller Ladders; Sue Gomez, marketing customer service manager for Zircon Corporation; Jim Brewer, marketing manager for Freud; Jim Poluch from The Eastwood Company; Jim Richeson, president of STA-PUT Color Pegs, Inc.; Bill Cork, public relations manager for the Plano Molding Company; Jeff Noland, president of HTP America, Inc.; Kim Garretson for DAP, Inc.; Matt Ragland, marketing manager for Empire Brushes, Inc.; Peter Wallace, senior vice president for McGuire-Nicholas, Inc.; Thomas Marsh, vice president of marketing, and Daryl Hower, business manager for Leslie-Locke, Inc.; Mike Cunningham, General Cable Co. (Romex®); Victor Lopez, techinal service representative for Behr Process Corporation; Greg Hook, communications manager for Plumb Shop; Mario Mattich, director of public relations for Leviton Manufacturing Company, Inc.; Ruth Tudor, product publicity manager for NuTone; Bob McCully, Vice president of sales and marketing for Power Products Company; Marty Sennett for DuPont Tyvek; and Beth Winfermantel, marketing communications manager for Weiser Lock.

Plenty of hands-on help was needed during photo sessions and project activities. For their patience and hard work, I thank Jim Yocum, Brian Lord, Bob Greer, and George Ramos. Working alongside these fellows was not only rewarding, but entertaining. Van and Kim Nordquist from Photographic Designs did an outstanding job developing film and printing hundreds of photographs. I appreciate the extra time they took to make sure each picture turned out just right.

I want to thank my wife, Janna, for her help in designing building plans with Autodesk Retail Products computer software, picking up building materials, assisting with photo needs, and processing paperwork. Our children pitched in as needed too. So thank you, Joey, Shannon, Michele, Jake, Terri, Steve, Whitney, Tyler, Kirsten, Courtney, Brittany, Adam, Matthew, Ashleigh, Bethany, Luke, and Nicholas.

Finally, I want to thank Kim Tabor and Stacy Pomeroy from TAB/McGraw-Hill for their continued support and enthusiasm for this book project. Their assistance and encouragement have been, and continue to be, refreshing.

A VAST majority of residential homes are structurally built with wood—*wood-framed*. Many are wood-sided and have wood-shake shingles, wood-framed windows, and wood panels inside. Most of the tools and equipment featured in this book are designed to cut, drill, shape, or otherwise make pieces of wood conform to specific applications. Therefore, one can easily surmise that wood and wood products are very important commodities for do-it-yourself homeowners.

A huge controversy has been going on for some time between wood industries and environmental organizations. Both sides have valid concerns. It is my contention that serious and practical compromise will lead to realistic solutions that will accommodate the best interests of everyone.

Wood-products industries have been actively involved with conscientious forest management for years. Millions and millions of new trees are planted each year to make wood a truly renewable resource. You are encouraged to write to the Western Wood Products Association, American Plywood Association, and the Cedar Shake and Shingle Bureau to learn

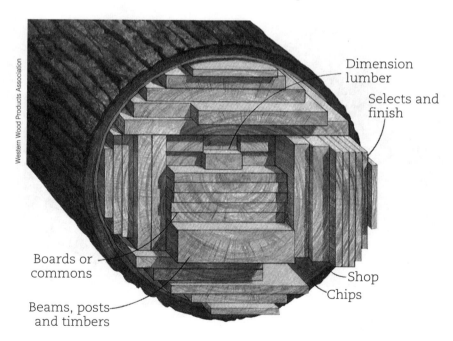

Western Wood Products Association

Dimension lumber

Selects and finish

Boards or commons

Shop

Chips

Beams, posts and timbers

more about this very important and timely issue and what is being done to preserve our environment, at the same time providing for our building, remodeling, and home-improvement needs. I am certain you will be impressed by the information available and astonished to learn of the many facts presented.

Along with technical information, the Western Wood Products Association, American Plywood Association, and Cedar Shake and Shingle Bureau offer building plans and decorative design ideas for all sorts of home-improvement endeavors. They range from structural building techniques and outdoor furniture to storage units and kitchen islands. Costs vary: Some pamphlets are free; others might cost up to $2.50.

Sheets of plywood are used for numerous applications. Many walls and roofs are sheathed with plywood. Some cabinets and storage systems are constructed of plywood, oriented strand board, or COM-PLY, then faced with another material. Plywood is generally available in 4-by-8-foot sheets that measure from ⅛ inch to 1¼ inches thick.

American Plywood Association

Cedar shakes are split to give them a
rugged-looking appearance.
Cedar shingles are sawn, which
makes them appear smooth.
Properly treated Certi-Guard
cedar shakes and shingles
offer fire resistance, as
proven by Underwriter
Laboratories tests.

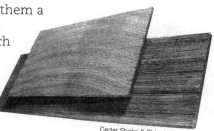

Cedar Shake & Shingle Bureau

Roof peaks require special roofing-material
caps that extend down both sides from
the top. These caps prevent water
from penetrating gaps between
otherwise regular flat shakes or
shingles that butt together at angled
peaks or hip joints.

Lumber yards and home-improvement centers often carry wide
selections of literature by wood-product manufacturers that
explain how to install and secure their specific types of wood
materials such as hardwood floors, siding, paneling, and so on.
Be sure to read, understand, and closely follow instructions.

ADVANCES in technology during the past few decades have introduced a new way of living for many people; folks 30 and more seemed to do a lot more of their own home-improvement and repair projects years ago. Perhaps children of earlier eras were taught to work with tools by parents or relatives because there were no computers or video games to occupy their time. High schools may have offered more shop opportunities because jobs at the time were more focused around industry and construction.

Today many high school and college graduates are well versed in computers, robotics, and technical skills rather than hands-on work involving tools and machines. Since their knowledge of home-improvement tools and equipment is limited, they are forced to hire professionals to fix or remodel things they could have done themselves—if only they had the tools and the know-how to use them *safely*.

This book has been designed as a source of primary information for homeowners and other do-it-yourselfers who want to learn about tools and equipment—what they are designed to accomplish, how they are intended to be used, and where they can be found. An appendix at the end of this book lists the names, addresses, and telephone numbers of numerous companies that manufacture and distribute the tools and equipment covered on the following pages. You are encouraged to call or write for catalogs and more definitive information.

Safety

Personal safety must be a serious and fundamental home-improvement and do-it-yourself consideration at all times. This fact cannot be overemphasized! Thousands and thousands of people have been injured or killed as a result of using power tools inappropriately, haphazardly, or without safety guards properly positioned; working in awkward positions on ladders; not paying close attention to conditions on roofs; working around live electrical wires; and so on.

Failure to wear eye protection accounts for thousands of eye injuries every year. Tool and equipment users can generally avoid such eye injuries by wearing safety goggles or full face shields. Manufacturer recommendations about wearing eye protection are printed or embossed on almost every tool distributed. Have plenty of goggles available so that every do-it-yourself helper is outfitted. Remember to peel off protective plastic films from both the inside and outside of new goggle lenses before using.

You must wear respiratory protection whenever working in dusty or polluted atmospheres, as when sanding, grinding, or painting. Paper dust masks are inexpensive and readily available at hardware stores, home-improvement centers, and lumber yards. Cartridge-type respirators, also readily available, are recommended for dust or paint-spray operations, which create heavy pollution conditions. Product and tool labels for items that could lead to heavy concentrations of airborne contaminants include specific information and recommendations for the use of certain types of respiratory protection.

Many of the power tools you will be using create loud noise. Therefore, invest in some type of hearing protection. Earmuffs,

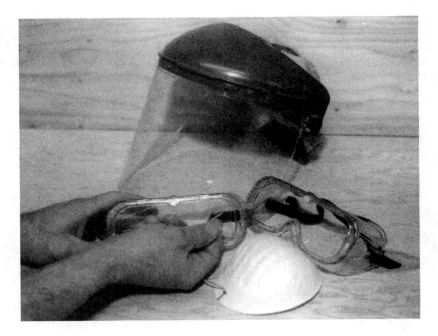

like these from Harbor Freight Tools, are excellent. Purchase more than one set and store them along with your goggles next to tools and pieces of equipment so that they are always on hand when needed. Extra sets are great for those times when more than one person is working in your workshop or close to operating equipment.

The installation of ground fault circuit interrupters (GFCIs) should be considered for all workshop electrical circuits. These safety devices quickly react to unusually high electrical flows to shut down power equipment immediately and prevent potential electrocution hazards. GFCIs are commonly installed as electrical outlets in bathrooms and other places where water supplies are located. In addition to GFCI outlets, GFCI extension cord sets are available through electric-supply stores and most home-improvement centers. GFCIs will sense increases in electrical current, whether due to water or other short-circuit problems, and cut off the flow of electricity before regular circuit breakers have time to react.

Always read and fully comprehend all operating instructions that accompany tools and equipment. Failure to follow directions can lead to disaster. Note maximum revolutions per minute (RPM) limits on tool attachments and compare those ratings with the RPM listing on power tools. Never use an attachment with an RPM rating less than that of the tool you

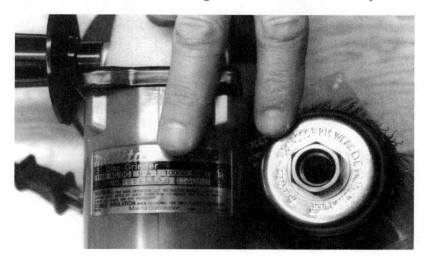

want to use it with. Grinding wheels, wire brushes, sanding disks, and similar accessories can break apart if their maximum RPM limits are exceeded. Make sure the power supply to tools is always disconnected while changing attachments.

Slide compound saws, miter saws, and other large power tools commonly feature bolt holes on their bases. Use these to secure tools to workbenches or tables with sturdy bolts, nuts, and washers. If you expect to move chop saws from your workshop to different sites as tasks dictate, consider using wing nuts for convenience. Keep a particular sheet of ¾-inch plywood on hand with holes drilled in it to match your saw's bolt holes. Use heavy-duty clamps to secure the plywood and its braces to sturdy sawhorses before bolting down saws.

Saw blades, router bits, drill bits, shaper heads, and planer blades are quickly dulled or destroyed by metal obstacles. In addition, nails, screws, staples, or embedded rocks hit by high-RPM cutters could easily shatter and send flying debris all over—a tremendous hazard. Cutting utensils like blades and bits can also be damaged to the point where fragments are thrown off at exceptionally high speeds. Therefore, always inspect wood and remove foreign materials before cutting, drilling, shaping, routing, planing, or conducting a similar operation.

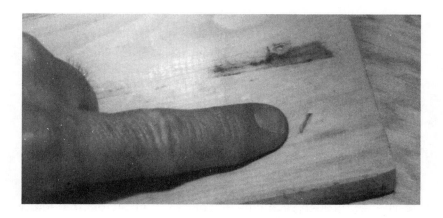

Extension cords can pose tripping hazards around any work site. Use cords that are long enough to reach electrical outlets easily, with plenty of slack to spare so they can be positioned to run away from the back sides of tools, equipment, and work areas; along walls; secured over door openings; and so on. The male ends of power-tool cords can be secured to the female ends of extension cords with a simple loose square knot to prevent them from coming apart.

Extension cords should always be at least the same size as or larger than the power cords for tools they supply. You wouldn't expect a ⅜-inch-diameter garden hose to supply a ¾-inch hose

to its maximum capacity, so don't expect a skinny household extension cord to safely supply the electrical needs of chop saws, table saws, drills, and the like. Lightweight extension cords attached to heavy-duty power tools will be overtaxed and get physically hot, possibly hot enough to trip circuit breakers or start a fire. In addition, inadequate extension cords can cause damage to power tools by not supplying them with the electricity needed for optimum performance.

Extra-long extension-cord runs should be made with cords bigger than the power-tool cords they supply to safely carry electrical current over long distances and overcome any extra resistance through such long extensions. Contractors frequently rely on heavy-duty extension cords that span 100 feet from a power generator to work sites. These cords are generally twice as big as those on circular saws, drills, and so on.

Personal safety must never be taken lightly. You and your family have decided to complete home-improvement tasks yourselves to save money and gain the personal satisfaction that goes along with jobs well done. While ensuring that you maintain safe work practices for yourself, do not overlook those family helpers waiting in the wings. They must also wear eye, hearing, and respiratory protection whenever exposed to hazardous conditions. Instruct them to stay away from power-equipment operations until tools are turned off and unplugged.

Always be alert to the locations of helpers during any sawing operation. Ensure that nobody, including yourself, is positioned in line with saw blades. Powerful, high-RPM blades on miter saws, table saws, radial arm saws, and circular saws are capable of throwing wood fragments at extremely high speeds. Chunks of wood thrown by large saw blades have been known to penetrate walls!

Warning: Read and understand all tool and equipment manufacturer operating instructions and safety guidelines before using tools or equipment. Then make absolutely certain all tool and equipment safety guards and features are properly positioned and personal safety gear donned before using tools or equipment.

Common hand tools

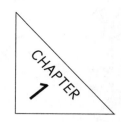

Hᴀɴᴅ ᴛᴏᴏʟꜱ are most generally regarded as implements powered by users' muscles as opposed to electrical outlets, batteries, or compressed air. Some of the more common hand tools are screwdrivers, pliers, wrenches, sockets, and ratchets.

Slotted screwdrivers feature a straight flat tip that fits into a slot on top of slotted screw heads. Phillips screwdrivers have tips that look like plus signs.

Slotted and Phillips screwdrivers are available in different sizes—thin tips for small screws graduating to large thick heads for big screws. Use whichever size best fits the screw head. Screwdriver tips that are too small for screws will either suffer chip damage or strip out screw-head areas. Screwdriver tips that are too big will simply not fit into smaller screw heads or tend to strip out a screw head's outer circumference.

Do not use screwdrivers as prying tools. They are not designed for such work. Strained under the pressure of leveraged prying, screwdriver tips may chip off, or entire shafts can be severely bent.

Getting into tight spaces with a regular screwdriver is not always easy; sometimes it is just impossible. Projects that involve the use of a slotted or Phillips screwdriver in a confined space may be best accommodated with a Yankee screwdriver.

Both handy Yankee screwdrivers at the bottom of page 2 feature two heads; one size on each side. A ratchet mechanism is operated by a lever to loosen or tighten screws without having to lift off and reposition the tool after each turn.

Another type of screw head commonly found on tools and machinery is called an Allen head, or hex head. Some Allen or hex fasteners are large enough to be called bolts. Instead of a single-slot or cross-slot head design, these units incorporate a six-sided hole that Allen wrenches or hex keys fit into. Ranges

Screwdrivers and hex and TORX keys

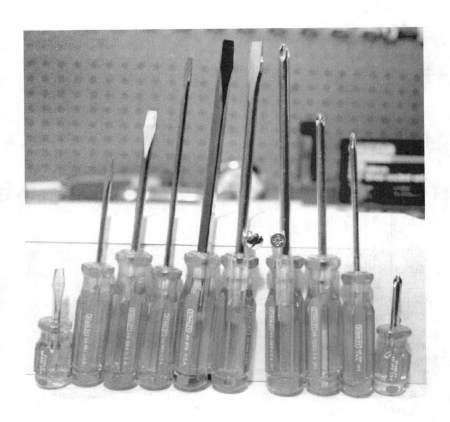

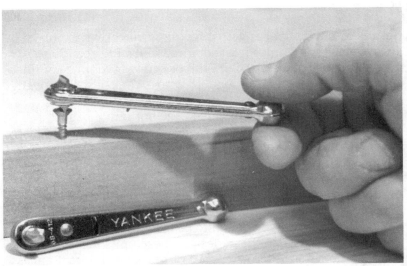

of hex sizes are used for various screw-bolt applications, depending on the size of the things being held together by them. Thus, Allen wrenches and hex keys are available in different inch (American) and metric sizes. You can purchase them as individual tools or attached together as units.

TORX is another screw-head variation developed just a few years ago. TORX tools feature a six-pointed tip that fits into TORX screws and bolts that have a six-notch design. Like Allen and hex wrenches, TORX bits come in different sizes. In lieu of inch or metric dimensions, though, TORX sizes go from a small T-10 through T-15, T-20, and T-25 to a large T-30.

Some special applications feature TORX fasteners with a pin that sticks up in the middle of the TORX hole. This design is intended as an antitheft measure. To loosen or tighten such fasteners, you must use a special TORX key with a hole in the middle of its shaft.

Wrenches

Wrenches are designed to loosen and tighten nuts and bolts. They are available in a wide range of sizes in inch and metric dimensions. A box-end wrench features a fully enclosed tip that fits completely over nuts and bolts. The straight sides inside this end make contact with all of the fastener's sides for a positive grip.

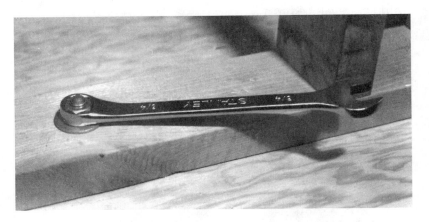

An open-end wrench differs from a box end in that a section of it has been cut out. This feature allows the open end to slide onto nuts or bolts as opposed to being placed over them before positioning.

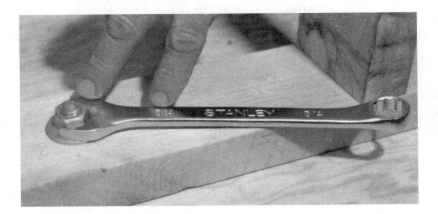

Wrenches are available in different styles. Those that feature a box end on one tip and an open end on the other are called *combination* wrenches. The box and open ends are the same size. Wrenches with two open ends are called *open-end wrenches*. Each open end will be a different size: 7⁄16 inch at one tip and ½ inch at the other; ⅝ inch and ¾ inch; 12mm and 13mm; 15mm and 17mm; and so on. The same is true for *box end wrenches*; each end will be a different size.

Although they may look nothing like combination, open, or box-end wrenches, *pipe wrenches* are wrenches nevertheless. These hand tools are designed to be used on round objects like pipes and extra-wide nutlike flanges and caps frequently found on plumbing fixtures and piping. The teeth on pipe wrenches are tooled to allow the jaws to grab onto objects and tighten as the tool is rotated in a handle-down direction. They won't work nearly as well, if at all, when the handle is lifted upward when the head has been placed down.

Ratchet and socket sets are handy tools. They perform the same function as wrenches (loosening and tightening nuts and bolts) but with a quicker and easier operation.

Ratchets & sockets

Ratchets feature a square pin onto which sockets are pushed. A lever or knob on the top of the ratchet head is maneuvered to remain fixed for tightening in a clockwise or counterclockwise direction. Depending upon the lever or knob setting, ratchets can be adjusted to lock-in for tightening, then ratchet in the opposite direction for repositioning. The socket never has to be lifted off the nut or bolt until the tightening or loosening is complete.

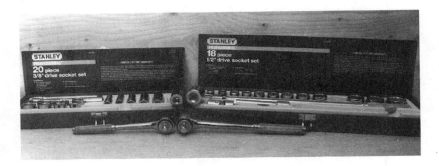

Ratchet and socket sets are sized by the dimension of the square pin on the ratchet and corresponding square hole on sockets. Small ¼-inch sets are perfect for lightweight jobs; ⅜-inch sets are ideal all-around applications. The ½-inch ratchet and socket sets are available for heavy-duty operations involving extra-large nuts and bolts.

Sockets are available in inch and metric sizes. They can be purchased separately but are much more economical in sets. Sockets have a square hole on one end for mounting onto specific ratchet drives (¼-inch, ⅜-inch, ½-inch) and a machined opening on the other end that fits over matching nuts and bolts. Another socket feature to consider is physical size—shallow or deep.

Shallow sockets work well on bolt heads and nuts that are not located too far down bolt shafts. *Deep* sockets are designed for applications where nuts need to be secured quite a way down long bolt shafts, where shallow sockets are just too short to reach far enough to make contact with nuts.

Sometimes you may find that a ratchet and socket combination would be good for loosening or tightening certain nuts or bolts but the fastener's location is such that the tool cannot be operated normally. This kind of dilemma might call for an *extension* and *universal-joint* combination affixed between a ratchet and socket.

Extensions are available in different sizes, from about 2 inches and up. Use them to reach up or down to nuts and bolts while keeping the ratchet in a more maneuverable position. A universal joint allows users to operate ratchets at other than 90-degree angles.

When nuts and bolts are torqued down excessively tight or torque specifications call for fasteners to be tightened more than normal, use a *breaker bar* in lieu of a ratchet.

Ratchet heads contain gears that can be stripped if forced beyond their capabilities. Breaker bars, on the other hand, are simple heavy-duty levers equipped with a swivel drive onto which sockets are attached. They are designed for high-torque applications.

A Makita cordless ratchet wrench makes loosening or tightening fasteners like mudsill-anchoring J-bolt nuts even easier. The push of a button is all it takes to activate the head and rotate sockets. To reverse direction, simply pull the square drive out from the head and insert it from the opposite side. This tool can also be used like a normal ratchet for obtaining higher torque ranges.

Many Makita cordless tools use identical batteries. Users may take a battery out of a compatible tool and use it to power a tool while the battery is being recharged. Such an occasion might occur when a ratchet wrench is needed outdoors during daylight hours and you don't need a portable fluorescent light. This system works well, especially with Makita's one-hour Fast Chargers.

The batteries for cordless power tools must be of the type and voltage recommended by the tool manufacturer. Never use one brand of battery with another brand of tool. Battery voltage and design must be compatible with the tools they are expected to power. Attempting to use a Makita battery in another brand of tool, for example, could quickly result in damage to both units and injury to users.

Regular pliers look a lot like scissors, but they grab things as opposed to cutting them. They will hold on as long as you maintain a firm grasp. When adjusted and applied properly, *Vise-Grip pliers* lock on to objects and stay put until their release lever is depressed.

Pliers

Vise-Grip pliers are available in a number of sizes and jaw configurations such as, regular, long nose, and bent nose. These tools are perfect for loosening stripped (rounded-off) nut or bolt heads, rotating small pipes, and numerous other tasks.

Along with Vise-Grip pliers, American Tool Companies offers completely different-looking tools based on the same type of locking system. Included is a large selection of various-size jaw clamps, welding clamps, bar clamps, and even a *locking chain clamp* that is perfect for lots of plumbing needs. See next page.

Although most people may regard pliers as tools to grab and hold things, there are other types designed for much different applications. Take Stanley *Jobmaster pliers*, for example. They can cut electrical wire, strip insulation, shear small screws and bolts, crimp terminals, and still be used like normal pliers with their nose jaws.

When you need to repair an electrical-cord end or install a new plug on the end of a power-tool cord, use a Makita cordless screwdriver and Stanley Jobmaster pliers for a quick, simple, efficient repair. The cordless screwdriver comes with a slotted bit and a Phillips bit. The charger is small and simply plugs into a standard electrical outlet.

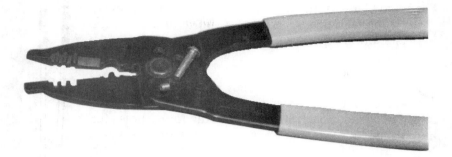

Just about everyone knows that shovels are made for digging holes. However, certain shovel designs used for appropriate maneuvers can make various dirt-moving or digging tasks much more efficient and easier to accomplish.

Structron Corporation offers a full line of heavy-duty fiberglass-handled shovels and other digging and landscape implements. The company's short D-handled shovels are available in square-point and round-point models. Their size and D-handle design makes digging in confined areas much more efficient and comfortable.

Square-point shovels work well for scraping dirt off smooth surfaces, squaring up footing trenches, leveling off concrete pad sites, and other jobs where flat shovel blades may be useful. Round-point shovels work better for digging holes and ditches, turning up soil for gardens, and other earth-moving tasks. Long-handled shovels are best maneuvered in open areas with plenty of working room.

Structron Corp.

Digging slim trenches for the installation of plastic drain pipe is a lot easier to accomplish with a trenching shovel than with a regular round-point model. Structron offers two blade sizes with their model—4 inches wide by 12 inches long and 5 inches wide by 12 inches long. With a 48-inch handle and a steeply angled blade, trenching shovels are great back savers for those who need to dig water-runoff drains or insert plastic drain pipes to divert water from gutter downspouts.

Post-hole diggers can most easily be described as tools that look like two shovels attached together. These tools are most commonly used to dig round holes for fence posts. Even though many do-it-yourselfers prefer to fill in around fence posts with concrete, the holes should be as tight as possible while allowing room for posts, concrete, and packed-down dirt. The reason for attempting to maintain straight vertical and undisturbed sides around post holes is to maximize post stability. Holes with crumbling walls or extra-wide openings make it very difficult to compact soil around posts or require more concrete for filler than normally needed. Without a post-hole digger, it is most difficult to achieve stable post holes.

Other outdoor tools

A regular garden hoe features a flat solid blade used for churning up soil and uprooting weeds. A *mortar hoe* is distinguished by holes in its blade.

Holes in the blades of mortar hoes accommodate users while they mix dry batches of mortar or cement with water. Once these mixes start to become more creamy, some material will flow through the holes as users continue to push and pull tools back and forth to blend cement and water. The reduced resistance on mortar hoes makes mixing jobs a lot easier and less strenuous.

You may not have given much thought to garden-rake designs until attempting to landscape an entire yard. Wide-spanning and rather lightweight *leaf rakes* do a great job of gathering leaves and twigs but fall short when it comes to raking rocks, clods, and other heavy yard debris.

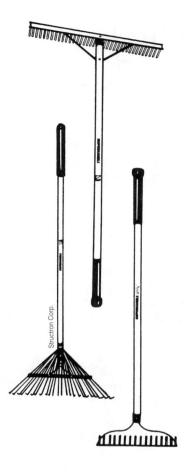

Structron Corp.

On the other hand, wide, multi-pronged reinforced *landscape rakes* do an excellent job of collecting all sorts of yard debris. *Bow rakes*, although not as big or rigid as their landscape counterparts, also work well for heavy-duty raking needs. Both of these models are designed for heavy raking chores in dirt. Used on grass, their prongs will tend to dig in, making them difficult to maneuver.

Accessory hand tools

Novice do-it-yourselfers may be somewhat familiar with common hand tools like screwdrivers, wrenches, pliers, ratchets, and sockets but may not be aware of the assortments of accessory hand tools.

The tools listed in this chapter are just some of the many hand-operated implements that you can use to facilitate home-improvement tasks and make them easier with more efficient results. Look through a Harbor Freight Tools catalog or browse through the tool sections of any home-improvement center or hardware store to get a better idea of what is out there.

Pry bars and nail pullers

Hammers are designed to strike things and occasionally to pull nails. Too much nail pulling will generally result in broken hammer handles. In lieu of using your claw hammer to pull nails, choose one of any number of claw-tipped *ripping (pry) bars*, dedicated *nail pullers*, or *offset-pattern ripping chisels*. These heavy-duty tools can hold up much longer than you can when it comes to pulling lots of nails, ripping boards apart, and doing other demolishing or remodeling work. Remember to wear eye and face protection while engaged in such rugged work.

To pull nails that have already been set close to wood surfaces, use a hammer to gently tap the claw end of a nail puller under the nail's head for a good solid grip. Pry up the nail ¼ inch or so until you are able to get the claw end of the tool under the nail for more leverage. Place a block of wood under bar ends for more leverage as nails begin to pull out farther. Beveled nail slots (holes) located at the wide ends of some nail pullers will allow users to pry in an upward direction for more control. Again, think about personal safety when pulling nails. Most of the time, nail pulling follows demolishing efforts where eye, respiratory, and hearing protection is mandatory.

Punches and chisels are handy home-improvement tools. Punches can be used with light hammer taps to push out sliding connector pins from appliances during repair, line up gears or bushings, or make center punch guides on metal before drilling.

Punches and nail-screw sets

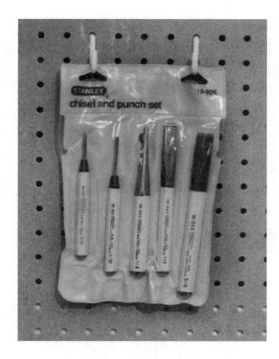

Cold chisels are designed for rugged use—to chip out slight concrete ridges or bend over thick metal tangs. Exercise caution when using cold chisels by wearing eye protection and good leather gloves.

TECHNICAL COLLEGE OF THE LOWCOUNTRY
LEARNING RESOURCES CENTER
POST OFFICE BOX 1288
BEAUFORT, SOUTH CAROLINA 29901-1288

Ordinary nail sets look like minipunches. Their flat tip is placed against finishing-nail heads, and the base is struck with a hammer to drive nail heads below wood surfaces. Those holes are then filled with wood putty, sanded, and finished. The end results appear as though no nails were driven into wood.

Nail sets are available in different sizes to accommodate various nail-head dimensions, slim set tips for small finishing nails, and larger set tips for bigger finishing nails.

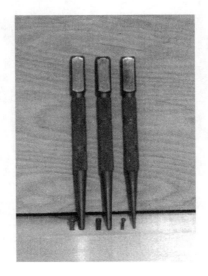

Anytime you plan to strike a metal hammer head against another metal object, there is a chance that metal burrs or chips could flake off either tool and strike you in the eye. Avoid those types of injuries by following tool manufacturer's recommendations (as engraved on hammer heads) and wear safety goggles.

Another type of nail set is designed to prevent accidental mishaps where sets slide off nail heads and gouge wood. These tools are called *self-centering nail sets.*

A spring-loaded pin is located inside the self-centering nail set. The tip that makes contact with nails rests a short way into the tool's body. As you should with any finishing nail you intend to set, leave the top ⅛ inch to ⅜ inch exposed; this also reduces chances of hammer blows striking and marring wood surfaces. Set the tool over the nail, then strike the top part of the nail set's pin with a hammer to drive nails into and below wood surfaces.

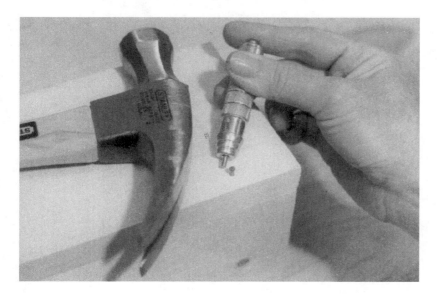

Drive nail heads 1/16 inch to ⅛ inch below wood surfaces to leave a hole big enough to support wood-putty filler. Allow that material to dry, then sand to smooth perfection. Done correctly, final results should appear as if no nails were driven into your finished pieces.

Attaching hinges, catches, doorstops, and other hardware to wood accessories with small screws may not always be as easy as one initially expects. Hardware products in most cases must be attached square, plumb, and perpendicular to operate correctly. Trying to start small screws by hand using only your eyes as guides is generally doomed to frustrating failure. Instead of relying on your wits and keen sense of hand-to-eye coordination to install hardware, make use of a *self-centering screw-hole punch* for easy and accurate screw installations on the first try.

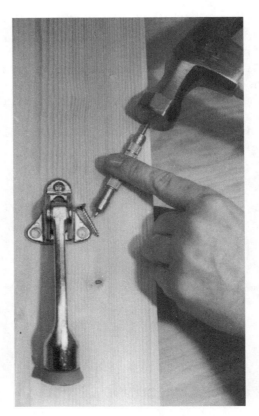

This screw-hole punch operates under the same basic principle as its cousin the self-centering nail set. The difference is in the shapes of pin and body tips. This tip is pointed so that it can quickly make a hole that is used as a definitive guide for screws. The body tip is beveled so that it can be quickly and easily centered in screw openings.

Once you have determined the exact location for your hardware item, use the screw-hole set to mark one screw's entry point. Insert that screw and tighten snugly but not quite completely. Then measure the hardware again and make any fine-tuning adjustments that may be needed. With that done and the hardware correctly positioned, mark and insert the second screw before continuing. This helps to secure hardware firmly before third or subsequent screws are installed.

Files

Some files are designed strictly for use on wood and soft materials, others for work on metals. For the most part, those with teeth that stick out unusually far are for wood. The ones with shallow and finer teeth are for metal. To be certain which ones are designed for what uses, read the information provided on labels or packaging.

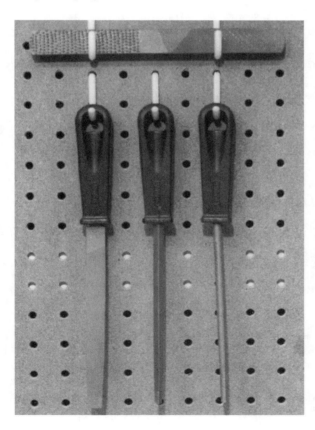

The top file, called a 4-*way rasp*, is used on wood and plastics and features four separate filing surfaces. On the left is a *6-inch mill bastard*; it is designed for general sharpening, polishing, and smoothing on metal. The 6-inch slim taper, in the middle, is used on metal to enlarge small openings, file notches, and smooth the edges of square holes. The *6-inch round bastard*, on the right, is used to smooth curved moldings, enlarge round holes, and so on.

Triangular-shaped files work well to help smooth out nicked screw and bolt threads, install new thread grooves on wooden broom handles, and similar tasks.

Surform files are used on wood, hard foam, and other relatively soft materials. Their sharp teeth work fast to remove lots of material with minimal passes. Blades are available in various sizes and shapes, including flat, half-round, and round. There are also a number of different handle selections to choose from.

A round Surform file works great for quickly enlarging holes and shaping decorative curved cuts in wood. The replaceable blade has a ⅝-inch diameter.

To replace a round Surform blade, first loosen the screw located at its handle (a Makita Cordless Screwdriver makes quick work of that). Then simply pull out the screw and dislodge the blade from its base. Consider wearing thick gloves while maneuvering the blade since some teeth could still be quite sharp. Again while wearing gloves, carefully insert a new blade into the Surform handle. Tighten the screw and check the blade to make sure it is safely secured.

Many home-improvement tasks require clean cuts on various materials, such as building paper, which is inserted between original subflooring, and new high-density particleboard underlay material.

Utility knives hold razor blades securely in place with a single screw that holds both halves of the tool tightly together. Razor blades have notches along their top sides that are placed into raised ridges that keep them from being forced into the knife body. Other models feature retractable blade mechanisms that can be easily operated to pull blades completely into the body when they are not in use. An open cavity between body halves makes a dandy storage area for spare razor blades.

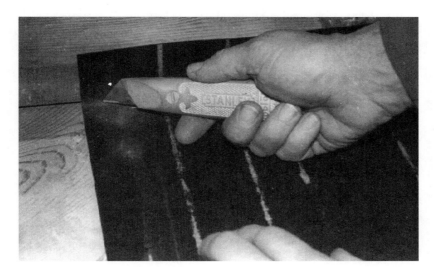

Wood chisels are very handy tools, especially when hanging doors, securing cabinets and cupboards, working with wood furniture, and a host of other tasks. Always check wood before using chisels to make certain there are no nails, screws, embedded pebbles, or other hard debris in the way. Wood chisels may be purchased separately or in sets that range from two or three tools to a full complement of nine.

The cutting ends on wood chisels are beveled or angled. This feature allows for a sharp edge that can quickly cut through most wood materials. Generally the beveled edge is held down to ensure wood is chiseled evenly. Should the flat part of chisels face down, the tool will tend to dig in deeper.

Practice with chisels before using them on precious hardwoods or expensive pieces of furniture that need repair. Information in chapter 11 will show you how to properly sharpen (hone) chisel blades.

Making straight marking lines across wide pieces of plywood or along walls is hard to do with just a pencil and short ruler. For those occasions where you need to mark lines along foundations for concrete pours or across full sheets of plywood, use a *chalk line*.

This tool incorporates a single string rolled around a shaft inside a tool body. On the outside, a lever attached to the shaft allows users to roll up string that has been pulled out. Powdered chalk is poured into the tool body through an access door. Chalk covers the string and stays attached to it until a taut string is snapped against an object. This snapping action causes chalk to come off the string and remain in place on the object being marked. Chalk washes and rubs off easily.

Chalk lines intended as cutting guides for hand-held power saws are fine for rough applications where cuts do not have to be exact. In lieu of an expensive panel-cutting saw, you could use a table saw with accessory supports, or enlist the help of an *all-purpose cutting guide.*

This expandable metal track guide can be adjusted to fit full-length (8-foot) sheets of plywood. Clamps hold the unit in place while the edge of a circular saw is operated adjacent to it. For added security, you can use additional clamps.

This type of guide requires users to compensate for the distance between a saw blade and the edge of a saw's base, which will ride against the guide. In other words, if you wanted to cut a sheet of plywood lengthwise in half into two 2-foot sections, do not place this guide on the 2-foot mark. First measure the distance from your saw's blade to the base edge that will ride against the guide, then move the guide over a distance equal to that measurement. Your saw's blade will rest at the 2-foot mark, right where you want the cut to be. Note: When making measurements on your circular saw, make absolutely certain it has been disconnected from its power supply.

Whenever cutting sections out of long pieces of plywood, be sure the plywood is securely supported underneath on both sides of the cut. Use four 2-by-4s—two on each side of the cut. Both sections will be equally supported during the cut and remain flat once the cut has been made.

Cutting thin strips of metal for heat ducts and other home elements of metal requires the use of special tools designed for those applications. Metal cutting snips and shears are available in different sizes, some with capabilities of cutting thicker materials.

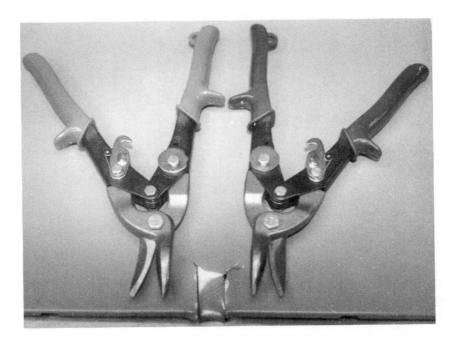

Prosnip aviation snips from the American Tool Companies, maker of Vise-Grip locking pliers and Quick-Grip bar clamps, come in three different models. One is designed for simple straight cuts. Another can make straight and right-turned cuts; a third cuts straight or toward the left. Plan to wear leather gloves while cutting metal. Sharp edges can quickly cut through skin. Wear safety goggles too.

In the last chapter, we discussed screwdrivers, hex keys, ratchets, and sockets. Here is another very handy fastening system to consider.

This Makita 25-piece ratchet set includes an easy-to-operate twist-type hand-held ratchet, slotted bits, Phillips bits, a socket adaptor, sockets, and six ballpoint bits for use on Allen (hex) screws. The ratchet is comfortable to maneuver, and its magnetic tip helps to hold bits securely in place. A small push lever near the ratchet's handle is moved back and forth for tightening or loosening.

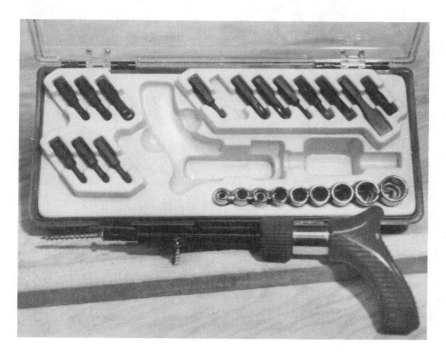

A home-improvement endeavor is seldom finished without the help of one or more clamps. Quick-Grip bar clamps are one of the most versatile types of clamps available today. This clamp comes in a variety of sizes ranging from 6-inch to 36-inch adjustable jaw widths. Use two of them together to span distances greater than 36 inches.

Quick-Grip bar clamps are tightened by just squeezing a pistol grip. Release tension with the depression of just one lever. They work great horizontally, vertically, and at any other angle.

Use clamps to hold cabinets together after spreading glue in preparation for wood-screw applications. Use them to secure wood to workbenches or sawhorses while sawing, drilling, or routing. Their versatility and simplicity is impressive.

Work that must be done around any electrical outlet or power source requires that power be disconnected before work begins. Situations of this nature are perfect for the use of cordless tools and lights.

The accessory hand tools discussed in this chapter are just a sampling of what manufacturers have to offer. Their catalogs are filled to the brim with lots of other styles, models, and additional accessory options. Call or write them for more information.

Measuring devices

"MEASURE it twice—cut it once." Sound advice that has been passed down from veteran carpenters and tradespeople to novices for years and years. The flip side to that statement goes something like "I'm going to cut this board just one more time, and if it's still too short, I'm going to quit!"

Quality tools that operate with perfection will accomplish home-improvement projects only if their guidelines and marks on boards and building materials are made and positioned accurately. Sawing, drilling, routing, nailing, screwing, and lots of other maneuvers rely upon well-placed and legible measurement marks that denote exactly where specific cuts are to be made, holes drilled, boards secured, pipes placed, and so on.

Professionals and do-it-yourselfers have lots of measuring-tool and equipment options. Squares, tape rules, plumb bobs, bevels, levels, and chalk lines are some of the more common and most heavily employed. Different types of squares, levels, and other tools are specifically designed for particular operations—for example *rafter* and *speed squares*, which are enhanced with lots of number and degree indicators to assist in making exact marks for cutting angled rafters and other support boards.

Tape rules

Numerous types and sizes of tape rules are also available. Various blades feature special kinds of measurement markings designed for specific applications—modular spacing rules for masonry work; metric dimensional units, and so on.

There are 50-foot and 100-foot tapes for those jobs where long measurements are necessary—fence building, concrete walkway-forming work, and so on. The long (over 30 feet) rule blades do not automatically retract; users must operate a crank to reel them back into their cases.

28   Home Improvement Tools & Equipment

Since most wood-frame walls are built with 2-by-4 or 2-by-6 studs placed 16 inches on center (OC), these tape rules usually feature red-block highlights every 16 inches. These marks help carpenters to recognize 16-inch OC locations while setting up wall-framing operations. This is especially handy once wall dimensions pass the 48-inch mark since the arithmetic for adding 16 inches to successive OC marks gets a little tough, especially for long walls: 48 + 16 = 64, 64 + 16 = 80, 80 + 16 = 96, and so on.

Squares

Pencil markings as cutting guides must be straight. This holds true for hand and precision power saws. The best way to make straight lines is with the use of a *square*. The Stanley professional combination square is just one tool ideal for such applications. Its base can be adjusted along the blade to accommodate different board widths. A 45-degree angle feature is handy for jobs requiring such cuts. A small bubble level is built into the base, along with an easily removable *scratch awl* that may be used in lieu of a pencil.

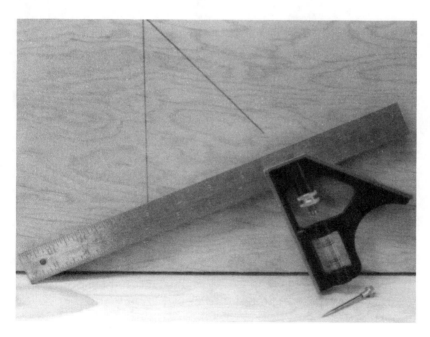

Another kind of handy square is the Makita Speed Square. Although it is not adjustable to various lengths, it can be used on one side of a wide board, then flipped over to the other side to accommodate 90-degree, 45-degree, and protracted line markings on boards up to about a foot wide. This tool includes many numerical markings designed to assist users in making specific marks and lines to use as cutting guides on roof rafters.

To learn how numbers and related marks on this square are applied to various building procedures, Makita includes a definitive booklet with each new Speed Square, including a wealth of information on how to measure and mark rafters for cuts to fit all sorts of roof designs from hips and valleys to ridges and dormers.

For integral rafter work involving large dimensional lumber like 2-by-10s and 2-by-12s, you might consider using a larger rafter square. The Stanley professional rafter square has a body 24 inches long with a tongue that measures 16 inches. It is much too big to fit into any toolbelt pocket. Embossed numerical graduations and figures are used to calculate precise cutting angles for rafters of all kinds. Like the Makita Speed Square, this tool comes with an informative booklet that describes exactly how to use the embossed information featured on both of its working sides.

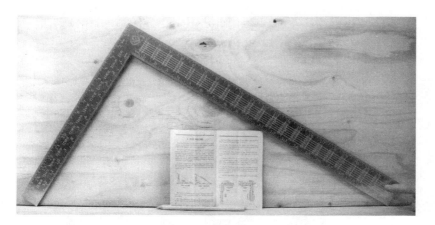

Designed for smaller woodworking jobs like making cabinets, cupboards, furniture, decorative accessories, and the like, a *bevel* tool can be quickly and accurately adjusted to any angle.

Loosen the wing nut, slide or move its arm to conform to the angle on a board end, tighten the wing nut, then use the tool as a guide to make a pencil line on another board so that you can cut it at exactly the same angle.

Along with matching angle cuts on precut boards, you can adjust bevel tools to any angle with help from a protractor. Be sure that center focal points are located at the bottom of the base so that that point of the protractor is positioned exactly at the base intersection of the bevel handle and its sliding arm. This will guarantee accurate readings.

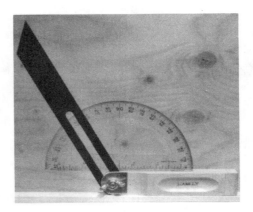

Gauges

A number of specialty gauges are available for intricate finish work. Some entail a single bar embossed with numbers in length increments, a slide marker that is set and locked at a desired length, and a scoring pin that protrudes from the bottom of the bar's tip. Called *marking gauges*, these tools are used to score straight lines on materials to assist precise cutting.

A *butt gauge*, on the other hand, is used to mark the positions and thicknesses of butt hinges on door casings. It can also be used to make similar marks for the installation of lock plates, strike plates, and the like.

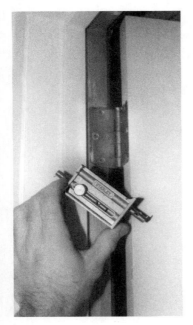

Gauges are of little help to anyone who does not know how to use them. This is why most tools come with definitive operating instructions. If you do not fully comprehend all directions after reading the instructions once, read them again. It may help to hold the tool up to an existing hinged door while reading directions to get a better perspective of overall door-hanging operations.

Most home-improvement projects involve installing objects that must be secured in positions that are horizontally and vertically level. This means exactly flat and straight upright. Off level just a little, home structures and their amenities will look awkward and in some cases may cause problems in later years, such as doors that will not close, windows that won't open, countertops that crack, and so on.

Long 4-foot levels are great for setting counters, walls, and most other large objects. Accurate level readings are easier to achieve on long levels. A center bubble vial is used to decipher horizontal levels; end vials are designed for vertical readings.

When the bubble is located exactly between the designating marks, you are assured that the object is level. Should a bubble be closer to a mark on one side than the other, the object is not level. To ensure that your level is reading correctly, place it on a countertop or against a wall and check the appropriate bubble position. Then twist the level around 180 degrees. Bubble positions for true levels should be exactly the same as those on the first reading. Levels range in length from just a few inches up to 8 feet. Levels over 4 feet long are generally reserved for brick and block masons and professional builders involved in huge construction projects.

At times, home-improvement professionals and do-it-yourselfers come across situations where the use of a level tool is not practical or feasible. One such case might be trying to determine certain points on floors located precisely under a particular part of a beam, ceiling light, or other such item. To help with these projects, take advantage of gravity and use a *plumb bob*.

Attached to a string suspended from the area above the floor on which you want to make a precise mark, heavy plumb bobs will hang perfectly upright; gravity guarantees it. A fine point at the tip of the plumb bob allows users to pinpoint precise plumb locations. Another use for plumb bobs is positioning framed walls. There may be circumstances where measurements have to be taken across ceilings to determine exactly where a wall should be secured. Measurements with a tape rule on floors may not be possible because of concrete foundation protrusions or other obstacles.

In those cases, after the framed wall top has been positioned, nail small pieces of wood to different places along the wall's top plate and let the plumb-bob string rest against them, one at a time. Make your marks at the plumb bob's point; measure in the same thickness of those small pieces of wood; then make your final mark. Those marks should be exactly plumb below the face of the framed wall to show where the wall's bottom plate should be secured.

Line levels, also referred to as *string levels*, are simple tools that can be exceptionally useful. Hooks on both ends are designed to fit over and be secured on line (string). With one end of a string attached to the top of a concrete form already secured in position, the other end is pulled tight, then moved up or down for installation of a parallel concrete form until the bubble on the line level reads level. The position of the string's loose end will determine where the top of the new concrete form should rest.

Outdoor leveling

Line levels are also used to determine uniform fence-post positions, straight and level lines for the installation of horizontal siding boards, and the like.

Although line levels are very useful and quite accurate when used correctly, *water levels* may offer more precise determinations.

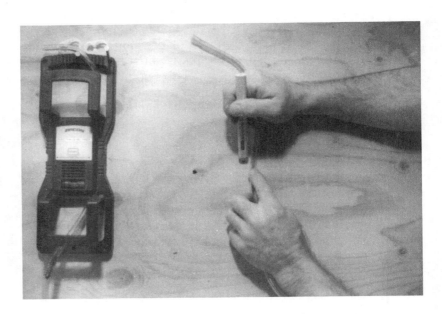

As long as the water in the level is not inhibited by air bubbles or foreign debris and the tool is operated correctly, water-level readings inside the box and at the free end of the clear hose will always be perfect. Water always seeks a perfectly flat and level plane. Undisturbed water surfaces always rest in a perfectly flat plane.

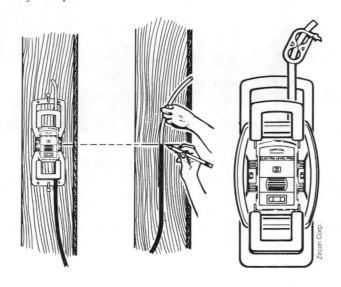

One person can use this tool by securing the box to a wall with its appropriate level mark lined up with a predetermined mark made on the wall. Stretch out the clear hose, filled with water according to directions, to the remote site where another level mark is needed. Bring the end of the hose down until you hear the box make a loud audible "beep." The level of the water at the hose's free end will be positioned exactly at the same level as the box's level mark.

After a water level, the next most accurate means of determining horizontal levels is with use of a *transit* or *engineer's level*.

These tools incorporate a telescopelike unit and a stick equipped with sets of measurement scales. Transits are intricate tools capable of numerous applications. Survey engineers use them all the time. Engineer's levels, on the other hand, are much simpler to operate because they are generally called upon only to determine grade levels.

Basically, once the viewing units are properly leveled, as determined by sets of bubble levels on their base, users look through the telescopelike part of the system toward their measuring stick, which rests on the ground in an upright position. After adjusting the focus, a set of cross hairs incorporated into the viewer will rest on a particular number on the stick. That number is then noted and used for all subsequent readings. The stick will be moved from place to place as dirt is removed or added and the transit or engineer's level rotated on its swivel base as needed. When all readings fall on the original stick measurement number, grade is guaranteed to be level.

Accurate measurements, level readings, and all other tasks undertaken to determine lengths, widths, and grades are very important. Simple mistakes made early during the construction of a room addition, workshop, or other structure will eventually become big headaches as these projects get closer to completion. Foundation walls that are not square will throw off wall framing, roof-truss installation, and other construction objectives. Cabinets, cupboards, and countertops installed off level will allow objects to roll off.

Always take your time when measuring or leveling to ensure accurate readings and markings before proceeding to subsequent operations.

Hammers, nailers, staplers, & screw guns

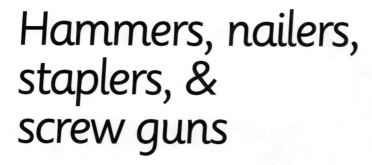

CHAPTER 4

The DIFFERENCE between a *hammer* and a *nailer* is power supply. Hammers drive nails by power supplied through a person's arm, wrist, and hand. Nailers receive their power from sources like air compressors, electricity, or compressed gas cartridges. *Staplers* are available in many different sizes. You may select from a number of models that are operated by hand, compressed air, or electricity.

Screw guns look very much like ordinary power drills. In fact, some *driver-drills* are designed for both operations. Dedicated power screwdrivers, however, are not generally set up for drilling.

Every Stanley hammerhead includes the words *WEAR SAFETY GOGGLES*. Heed this recommendation. Chips from nails, hammerheads, or other objects can easily be thrown toward your face and into one or both of your eyes. In addition, realize that hammers used to strike chisels, punches, wedges, and other implements, should have a face size ½ inch larger than the head of the tool being struck; a ½-inch cold chisel requires at least a 1-inch hammer face.

Enthusiastic do-it-yourselfers could have a field day outfitting their workshops with all sorts of hammer sizes and styles. Some of the biggest hammers you'll need are called *sledge hammers*. These big hammers are available with heads that weigh from 6 to 12 pounds. They are used to break concrete, brick, and the like. The *engineer's hammer* in the middle weighs 4 pounds and is great for driving stakes, pounding on cold chisels, and doing other heavy-duty tasks. The short-handled

Common hammers

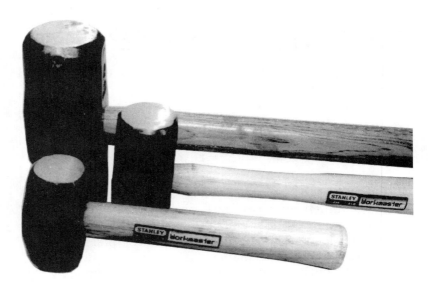

hand drilling hammer in front weighs 3 pounds and is used for many of the same purposes as the engineer's model.

Claw hammers are most commonly used to drive nails. Claw features have been designed for pulling nails bent during installation. These types of hammers are readily available in various weights, from a mere 7 ounces to 28 ounces. For most all-purpose applications, do-it-yourselfers generally find 16-ounce to 22-ounce hammers most versatile and easy to use; 26-ounce and 28-ounce hammers are heavy, especially when tackling big framing jobs that require lots of nailing.

Hammerheads come in two basic finishes: smooth and *milled checkered face* (wafflelike). Smooth types will not damage wood surfaces nearly as profoundly as the milled checkered face, nor will they peel the hide off of your fingers as dramatically in case you accidentally miss a nail and hit your fingers.

People use framing hammers with milled faces to nail studs and other rough-carpentry components where checkered patterns made on wood surfaces are of no consequence. The checkered face pattern on these hammers helps to prevent hammerheads from sliding off nails and ensure more solid nail-driving power with each stroke. Professional framers commonly prefer checkered faces because they don't have time to straighten bent nails and need to drive nails quickly to be most productive.

A smooth-faced 16-ounce fiberglass handle nail hammer is often ideal for lots of home-improvement tasks. A smooth face is gentle on wood surfaces, and the weight is quite maneuverable for most users. A curved claw makes pulling bent nails a little easier in some situations but more important, allows a bit more room behind it for maneuvering before hammer strikes. Optional ripping claws stick out the back of hammers in a straighter line, like that on the milled-face framing hammer.

Nailing hammers are available with different types of handles. Some are wood, generally hickory. Others are made of steel, fiberglass, and graphite. Although steel handles may last almost forever, they do not absorb much shock and can tire your hand, wrist, and arm rather quickly. Wood, fiberglass, and graphite handles do a much better job of shock absorption. Expect graphite-handled hammers to last the longest, absorb the greatest shock, and probably cost more than the others.

Lighter-weight smooth-faced nailing hammers are preferred for doing trim and finish carpentry work. Their size is easily managed for more complete control. When trying to select a hammer from racks and racks of various models and styles, pick up each one to determine how comfortable it is in your hand. Keep in mind the type of work you will be doing with the hammer—rough or finish carpentry, general fix-it tasks, and so on.

Huge hammers are *not* needed for finish-carpentry tasks like nailing support boards to cabinet or cupboard shelves. A 12–16-ounce hammer should be just right for this type of operation, nail setting, trim and molding work, picture hanging, and so on.

Heavy framing hammers used for intricate nail-setting tasks may cause nails to be set so far inside facing and trim that they actually lose their holding power. In this case, bigger is not better.

Nails need to be set only about $\frac{1}{16}$ inch to $\frac{1}{8}$ inch below wood surfaces, just enough to support filler material adequately. Lighter hammers also make it easier to make solid contact with nail sets and avoid accidental misses where hammerheads dent or gouge wood surfaces.

In addition to claw (nail) hammers, you will find many other types of hammers in home-improvement stores, hardware stores, and catalog houses like Harbor Freight Tools. *Ball peen* hammers have a regular striking head, but their rear head is rounded. These are used for striking punches and chisels and shaping metal. They are most commonly seen in auto-repair facilities, machine shops, and other such places. *Tack* hammers have very small striking heads on both front and back sides. Upholstery workers use them for installing tacks on furniture.

Hatchets are used by some professional framers. They like these tools for their heavy weight in driving big nails with just one or two blows. Blades are useful for ripping apart wood pieces to make them fit into certain positions. *Drywall hatchets,* much smaller versions of so-called framing hatchets, have striking heads rounded so that cupped indentations can be made fully around drywall nail heads that are sunk below drywall surfaces. Impressions in drywall are made to make room for a drywall "mud" covering, a process that hides drywall nails to make walls look and feel smooth. The hatchet end works great for cutting pieces of drywall out of the way, and a notch on the hatchet blade is for pulling nails.

Power staplers

The term *staple gun* generally refers to a hand-operated tool that features a large lever on top of its body that when forcibly depressed shoots staples with a loud *click. Power staplers,* on the other hand, are electric or compressed-air machines capable of shooting much larger and stronger staples with just the pull of a trigger.

Pneumatic staplers work well for securing plywood sheathing to studs and lots of other fastening jobs. Various models deploy different-size staples, from $7/16$-inch crowns to full 1-inch. Two

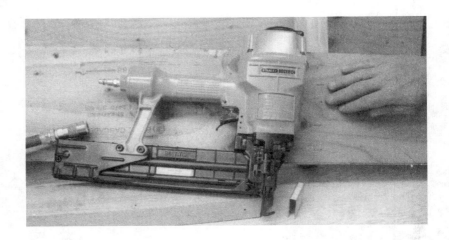

kinds of triggering systems are available with the Stanley Bostitch models. The *sequential trip* model requires operators to hold tools against the work before pulling the trigger. This makes accurate fastener placement easier. The *contact trip* model allows users to hold down the trigger so that every time the tip makes contact with a hard surface, a staple will be discharged. The contact trip mechanism makes it easy for operators to drive lots of staples in a short time but carries with it the problem of unintentionally discharging staples on tool recoils. Use extreme caution when operating such tools and wear safety goggles.

Almost all pneumatic tools used on a regular basis require lubrication once or twice a day. Just a few drops of *air-tool lubricant* is all that's needed. More than that will simply collect inside tools and spray out of exhaust ports. Lubricant is generally applied through air-hose inlets, although you must read your tool's operating instructions for exact directions. Air tools are normally sold without air-hose couplings, which must be purchased separately. Normally, male couplings are inserted into tools; air hoses are equipped with female ends. Apply Teflon tape to threads to ensure leak-free connections.

Staples are loaded into pneumatic staplers by pulling back a spring-loaded mechanism (pusher) that slides on a long shaft. With the pusher locked in its loading position, just place clips of staples on the shaft until it is full. Release the pusher so that

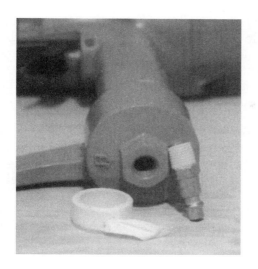

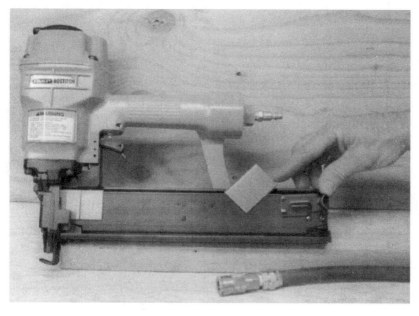

it will put force against staples to automatically feed the power head. Always be certain that pneumatic staplers have been disconnected from their air supply and that you fully understand operating instructions before loading.

One Stanley Bostitch pneumatic stapler features a means to adjust staple penetrating depths. The Dial-A-Depth adjustment must be made only when the tool has been disconnected from its compressed-air-supply hose. This feature allows users to sink staples completely below wood surfaces or allow staple crowns to remain visible.

To make a depth adjustment, open a small door on the side of the tool's tip mechanism. Inside is a knurled nut that is simply turned in one direction or the other to cause staples to penetrate work deeply or have staple crowns remain above work surfaces.

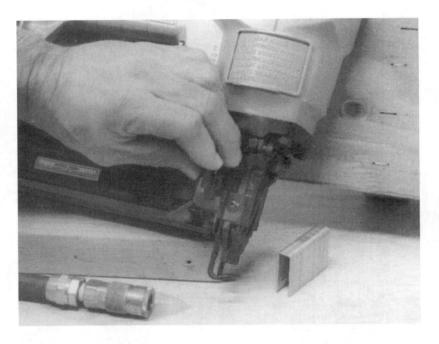

Most electric staplers are not nearly as powerful as their pneumatic counterparts, although they are capable of embedding staples completely into your skin. These smaller units are commonly used for securing insulation to studs, securing paper to sheathing, and so on.

The Stanley heavy-duty electric stapler-nailer has the capacity to discharge staples or *brads*. Brads work well for securing hardboard backing to cabinets, trim pieces to finish work, and other light nailing tasks. These tools commonly feature a very short cord, so expect to employ a quality extension cord.

The Campbell Hausfeld *stick-framing nailer* can drive nails from 2 inches to 3½ inches long. It makes quick work of framing wood-stud walls, securing deck material, and lots of other big nailing tasks. Nails used in this tool's magazine come in packs with nails secured together for easy loading. Employ a Campbell Hausfeld portable air compressor as a power supply, or use a heavy-duty air-supply hose connected to your workshop's stationary compressor.

Pneumatic nailers

Campbell Hausfeld's coil roofing nailer is ideal for roofing and sheathing jobs. Its magazine holds 120 roofing nails from ⅞ inch to 1¾ inches long, enough for an entire bundle of shingles before reloading. Be sure to read the operating instructions to determine appropriate air-pressure settings and supply.

For molding, trim work, and cabinets, consider using the Campbell Hausfeld 2½-inch finishing nailer. It operates off a minimal compressed-air supply, which is sufficient to provide enough power for countersinking 1¼-inch to 2½-inch finishing nails into hardwoods. A tool like this is perfect for those tough jobs where maneuvering a hammer is difficult because of confined access.

The Makita cordless Driver-Drill works great as a drill and a screw gun. It is equipped with an adjustment ring close to the tip that engages a clutch designed to halt screwing operations once a fastener has been sufficiently installed.

Screw guns

This clutch feature allows users to install screws to prescribed depths, a real asset when working with soft materials. The

tool's chuck is just like those featured on regular power drills. The chuck key is carried on the tool in a handy storage pocket. For drilling, simply rotate the adjustment ring until it lines up with *drill*. Then use it as you would any power drill. Be certain to wear safety goggles whenever using this tool.

Even with its adjustment ring positioned at a relatively sensitive clutch setting, driver-drill bits are driven strongly enough to cause hand injuries if the tool is operated contrary to its operating instructions. Therefore, be sure to read and follow directions closely and keep all loose items away from the tool's working tip—screws, other tools, extension cords, idle hands, arms, feet, and so on.

Installing screws in subfloors helps to reduce the chances of annoying squeaks developing. Use quality screws; wear goggles; and seriously consider good kneepads.

It is not uncommon for screw heads to break off as they are torqued into solid wood joists, especially during remodeling jobs on older homes where wood has hardened over time. Use the *reverse* feature on your driver-drill to pull out broken screws; then insert new ones next to them. If you don't, broken heads may eventually loosen and start popping up through vinyl or other floor coverings.

Dedicated *drywall screwdrivers* are equipped with a clutch that stops the tool's screwing head as soon as a preset torque limit is reached. This allows users to dial an exact depth for drywall screws so that they will penetrate drywall surfaces just enough to accommodate mud and tape operations.

The Makita drywall screwdriver is a comfortable size with balanced weight. A *reverse* lever is located at the tool's base, positioned just right for quick operation by a user's little finger. A belt hook, on top of the tool, comes in handy when you are finished screwing a sheet of drywall in place and need to retrieve and position another one that is located nearby.

Although Phillips bits are rugged, they eventually wear out. To help them last longer, be sure bits match the screw heads they will be used on. Replacing bits on this tool is quick and easy. Pull off the silver collar and simply pull out the old bit. New ones are just pushed in.

Be sure this tool is unplugged before making any adjustments. To adjust the clutch mechanism, push in and rotate the black collar located closest to the tool body, furthest away from the tip. Twist it slightly clockwise to lock it. Then turn the silver collar clockwise for maximum depth, counterclockwise to reduce it. As with any new tool, read and understand all operating instructions before putting it to work.

Power-screwdriver bits will generally not spin unless they are in contact with an object as the clutch inside this tool is disengaged. Once pressure is put against the tool's tip to engage the clutch, bits will spin as expected. To drive screws, pressure must be placed against power-screwdriver tips to engage the machine's clutch mechanism.

Drills & drill bits

ALMOST every home-improvement project will require holes to be bored in something. On the smaller side of the scale, finish-carpentry endeavors frequently call for tiny finishing-nail *pilot* holes to guard against splits in fragile wood trim. Graduating to the bigger side of the scale, heavy-duty *rotary hammers* and special carbide-tip drill bits are most often needed for boring holes in concrete.

Enthusiastic do-it-yourselfers with a keen interest in tools and accessories could easily outfit their workshops with a dozen different hand and power drills complemented with hundreds of drill bits of various sizes and styles. Practical homeowners can expect to be well served with a minimal selection of quality drills and bits as long as the tools and accessories they choose are appropriate for the job.

Hand drills

Boring holes in fragile wood trim, precious wood amenities, and other intricate components requires controlled and careful attention. The use of a *hand drill* for such operations will allow users to monitor work with great precision.

You do not need to apply much force behind hand drills; let the bit do the cutting. Take your time and be patient. Attempting to force bits and speed up their operation will hinder your overall objective—to bore perfect holes and limit risks of damaging wood surfaces.

Simply driving a finishing nail directly into a thin piece of wood can easily cause wood to split, especially trim. Experienced craftspeople drill *pilot holes* through which finishing nails are then inserted. Pilot holes are just slightly smaller than finishing-nail diameters; big enough to prevent wood splits but tight enough to give nails a chance to hold wood in place. Since pilot bits are generally quite small, you must resist the temptation to push down forcibly on hand drills because you can easily cause bits to break. This would result in the hand drill falling onto the workpiece to cause blemishes.

After drilling holes with your hand drill, operate the handle in a reverse direction to help bits pull out more easily. Insert nails partway and leave their heads sticking up so that a nail set can be used appropriately.

Larger hole boring requires a bigger drill and drill bits. This is where a *bit brace* and *auger bits* are useful.

Some bit-brace hand drills accept only certain types of drill bits; note the shaft ends on bits opposite their cutting tips. Others, like the one on the opposite page, also accept regular round-shaped drill bits. A knurled collar at the working end of the bit brace is simply hand-tightened to secure bits in place.

For boring any number of different-size holes in furniture, cabinetry, and other types of finish work, consider an *expansive bit*.

These bits are adjustable, as indicated by the screw, wide blade, and numerical indicators located at the base. Stanley's expansive bit comes with two blades, offering users a wide variety of size options.

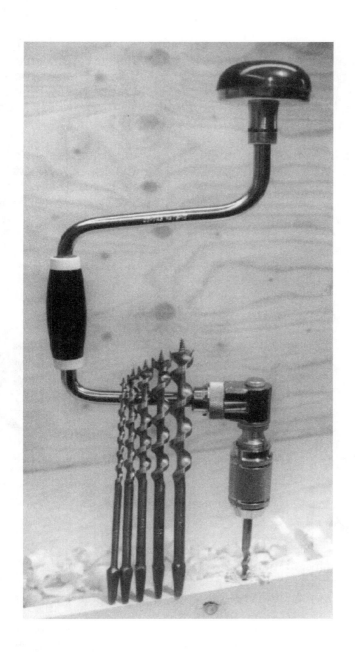

Power drills

The advent of variable-speed and reversible power drills has greatly increased the utility of power drills in finish carpentry and home improvement. Although hand drills remain most useful for intricate projects, conscientious power-drill users can expect excellent performance from any number of power-drill options.

A Makita ⅜-inch variable-speed reversible drill is ideal for almost all projects. Its powerful motor has a 0–1,200-RPM range. Use it for drilling in wood or sheet metal. The tool is well balanced and lightweight for comfortable handling. Note the handy chuck-key holder.

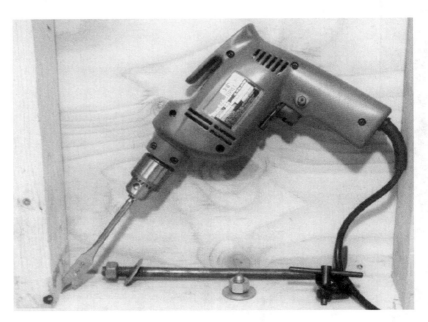

A "⅜-inch drill" designates the largest-diameter bit shaft that can be inserted into the tool's chuck. As opposed to a ¼-inch model, ⅜-inch units are designed to bore bigger holes with larger bits not only because of the chuck size but also a larger motor. Bits that bore holes larger than ⅜ inch can be used with these drills, but the part of their shaft that fits into the chuck must be tapered to no more than ⅜ inch. Bits with those tapers are available through home-improvement centers, hardware stores, and mail-order tool companies like Harbor Freight Tools.

Along with a wide selection of all-purpose power drills, Makita offers a ⅜-inch cordless angle drill. The right-angle design on this tool is exceptionally handy when users need to bore holes in tight spaces, as between wall studs. Notice how the angle drill is able to bore a straight hole in a stud, whereas the regular power drill would have to drill the hole at an angle.

Heavy-duty boring operations like drilling in concrete or through large timbers may require the use of a powerful ½-inch drill. As with other size drill motors, the ½-inch designation refers to the largest bit shaft that can fit into the tool's chuck as well as noting that the tool will be equipped with a motor that is bigger than ⅜-inch and smaller drills.

Because their motors are quite large, ½-inch power drills are normally designed differently than smaller models. Note the big D-handle at the rear and the perpendicular handle attached to the side of the tool. This configuration offers users a much more stable and controlled handling position. Be aware that ½-inch power drills are equipped with heavy-duty motors. The torque generated by them is tremendous, and all operators must be thoroughly familiar with the tool's operating instructions before putting them to work. As with all power-tool work, always wear safety goggles.

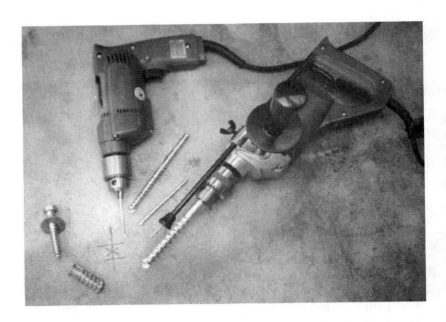

The long shaft alongside this Makita ½-inch drill is used as a depth gauge. While the tool is disconnected from its power supply, determine how deep you want a drill bit to penetrate the work. Loosen the rod's wing nut; adjust the rod to a location on the bit that corresponds to where you want it to stop. Then tighten the wing nut. Once the bit has penetrated to a designated depth, the rod will make contact with the work surface and halt boring.

The ½-inch right-angle attachment for Makita ½-inch drills is great for large boring needs in confined spaces. Regulating control of this powerful tool is assisted through a two-speed option—800 RPM for small holes and 350 RPM for large holes. You must still be aware of the tremendous torque generated by this tool. Always maintain a firm and secure grip on the tool, and make sure your footing is well balanced and stable.

Drilling holes in concrete, especially old concrete that has been around for a few decades, can be labor-intensive. Ordinary ⅜-inch and ½-inch drills that rely on high-speed twisting bits may require patience for some drilling jobs. You may find that drill bits will not last as long as expected. For those tough boring jobs, seriously consider the use of a Makita *rotary hammer* equipped with special *percussion bits*.

Rotary hammer

Rotary hammers combine the effects of a normal high-speed bit with the force of hammering blows. That combination allows these tools to drill through concrete and other hard surfaces quickly and easily, providing the appropriate bits are used. These tools are great for drilling through pressure-treated mudsills and concrete floors for the insertion of wall anchors.

Many heavy-duty rotary hammers are designed to accept specific bits equipped with unique shafts. Unlike ordinary chucks, which require a chuck key for tightening, these bits are equipped with splines that are engaged into rotary-hammer chucks with just the twist of the chuck's collar. Be sure to read and follow the tool's operating directions.

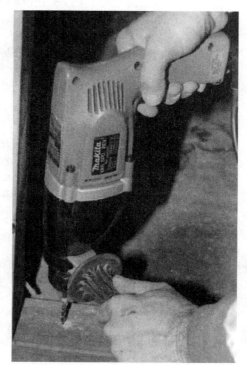

Regular twist-type bits will not work with this rotary-hammer chuck. The bit has slots on each side that are secured in the chuck when the chuck's collar is rotated to the lock position. Apply a small amount of grease to these bit shafts before inserting them into chucks. This is a safety and maintenance task that will prolong the life of the bit shaft and the chuck.

Rotary hammers are powerful tools that make quick work of drilling through tough surfaces. Seriously consider their use for remodeling chores like boring holes through interior wall studs and concrete foundation walls for the insertion of anchors.

Many basements have concrete walls that are bland to look at and offer little insulation or opportunity to hang pictures or other wall decorations. New interior walls for basements, finished like any other household wall, may offer a more pleasing atmosphere and an easier means to secure wall-mounted adornments. Once a hole has been bored through studs and into concrete walls, use any of a number of anchoring devices to mount studs to concrete.

One of the simplest employs a slightly sliding tapered fitting on the bottom of an anchor-bolt shaft. It snugs up significantly inside concrete holes as a nut is screwed down on the other end of the anchor bolt.

Makita's rotary hammer can be outfitted with a regular ½-inch chuck for normal heavy-duty drilling operations. An optional chuck adaptor, used to make the transition, has slots at one end and a screw shaft on the other. The slotted end is inserted and secured into the rotary hammer, and a ½-inch chuck is screwed onto and secured with the appropriate hex-head screw on the other.

Drill press

Precision drilling for intricate purposes is accomplished through the use of a *drill press*.

Drill-press units are available in many different sizes. This model from Harbor Freight is a *benchtop* type, which means it is designed to fit on top of a well-constructed workbench. Much larger *freestanding* units extend up to 5 feet and taller. Large drill-press machines are capable of much more heavy-duty and prolonged operations.

Harbor Freight Tools

Drill presses incorporate a head-mounted motor located behind the drill chuck. A series of pulleys and a belt are adjustable to accommodate various chuck speeds for drilling through different materials and thicknesses. Once work has been secured to the drill-press table, operators turn a spoke wheel that lowers the bit into the work for accurate boring. In addition to precision, drill presses equipped with specific guides can be used to bore identical holes on different pieces repeatedly; the tool's setup will remain unchanged. This is how professional furniture makers and other tradespeople make perfectly matched holes on stools and other items.

The Stanley bit brace and Makita rotary hammer may accept only certain bits with shafts made to conform to their chuck's design. Although most ordinary power drills utilize the same kind of cylindrical bit shaft, you must understand that various bit tips are designed for specific uses. In other words, don't expect to use a wood bit to drill holes in metal.

Drill bits

The Makita heavy-duty black-oxide 29-piece drill-bit set includes bits that range in size from $\frac{1}{16}$ inch to $\frac{1}{2}$ inch. These tools are designed for use on metal. They are equipped with a special tip that helps to reduce "walking," a condition where bits used on metal tend to move laterally across the work instead of penetrating straight ahead. Another way to prevent walking is to start out with a very small bit; then graduate to larger ones; or use a *center punch* to make an initial indentation in the work.

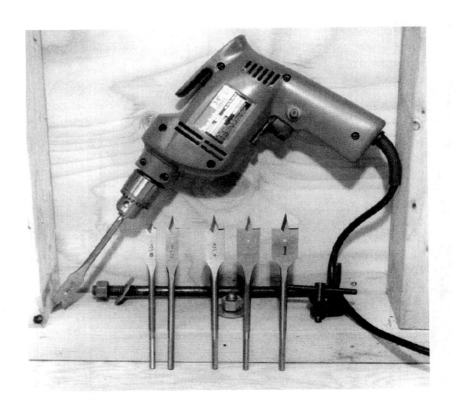

Although high-speed bits like Makita's black-oxide models can be used successfully on wood, you may have better success using bits designed for that work, especially when jobs require large bores.

Spade bits drill clean holes in wood, plastic, plywood, and similar materials. They work well for many light to medium tasks. Bit blades can be sharpened a number of times before bits are no longer useful. Using these bits for drilling completely through wood will generally result in numerous splinters and rough edges on the piece's back side. To avoid this, turn the work over as soon as the pilot point pokes through; then drill from the back of the wood toward the hole already established.

A hole in the blade of these bits can be used to assist efforts in pulling small wires through holes. This feature is handy while trying to "fish" electrical wires through walls during home remodeling. Never use bits in this manner while they are connected to a drill motor.

Boring holes in large timbers requires bits that are strong and long enough for the job. Such applications might be the installation of heavy timber planter boxes, small retaining walls, and so on. Jobs like these call for the use of *ship auger bits*. Note the unique design of these bits. As opposed to a solid shaft with flutes circling around it, ship auger bits are completely fluted. This feature allows quick and thorough wood-chip discharging.

Makita's tough heat-treated ship auger bits can cut through small nails and some other foreign materials commonly embedded in power poles, railroad ties, and other heavy timber pieces. Bits can be sharpened numerous times to guarantee long life, and their screwpoint tip works great as a self-piloting mechanism. Because of their shaft (shank) size and the depth of work expected from them, ship auger bits must be used with ½-inch drills.

Another means of drilling holes through wood is *hole saws*. These tools are perfect for jobs requiring clean, smooth cuts on both sides of a workpiece, as for door handles, locks, and so on.

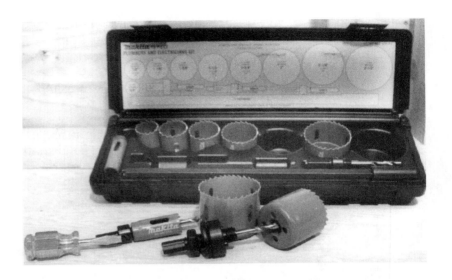

Individual units are secured to arbors that already have a pilot drill attached. A pilot drill is mandatory; it is the mechanism that allows hole saws a chance to get started in work initially and remain on course.

Some inexpensive hole-saw sets feature a set of grooves on their base unit to which saws are twisted into place. Others have threaded shafts onto which saws with threaded center sections are secured; the problem with those is that saw units become so heavily torqued down on top of their bases, they are almost impossible to remove.

Makita hole saws are equipped with four holes in their base (only two are used, but four are provided for adjustment purposes). Pins on the arbor base are loosened and moved down, then pushed up into base holes after saws are threaded onto arbors. Saws are not tightly screwed down. A little play is left so that they do not become torqued onto the arbor after use. The pins keep saws in place to avoid high-torque-tightening dilemmas and allow saws to function as viable cutters. You must read and follow operating instructions to ensure proper assembly and hole-saw usage.

During projects that involve plumbing, electrical, and other tasks, holes must frequently be drilled through heavy lumber for the installation of pipes, wiring, and the like. Since the lumber will eventually be covered, the appearance of drilled holes is of no consequence; therefore, consider using Makita self-feed bits for heavy-duty drilling operations requiring large holes.

Self-feed bits, tough tools designed for rugged work, can chew through wood quickly and accurately. Makita's models feature a double-ended screw point in the center of the bit. Threaded points help to pull bits into their work, and the double-end design allows users to reverse them as one end becomes dull. Extensions are available for jobs requiring extra-deep boring.

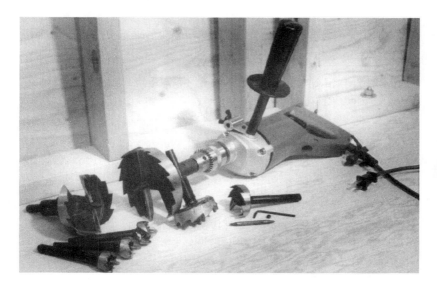

New self-feed bits are covered with a waxlike substance. This material protects against rust and helps bits stay sharp during storage and transit. Wear gloves and exercise caution while peeling this material off; new bits are very sharp. Don't forget to wear safety goggles.

When using a self-feed bit, be sure to maintain a very tight grip on your drill and maintain balance and complete control over the operation. These bits really dig into wood and can cause drill motors to twist with great torque. When using large bits, consider bracing the drill motor handle against a stud or other solid component to hold the tool in position.

Specialty drill bits are available in all sorts of sizes, shapes, and designs. You can even select some capable of drilling more than straight holes, such as Stanley's screw-sink 3-in-one set models.

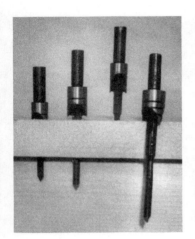

Along with drilling pilot holes for screws, these tools can countersink and counterbore. *Countersink* means that holes are wider at the top so that screws can fit flush with wood surfaces. *Counterbore* entails a wider and deeper hole so that an entire screw can be inserted past a wood surface, then covered with filler or a wood plug.

Wood plugs are common for furniture, hardwood floors, and other attractive wood objects where fastening screws must be hidden. Wood plugs in many different sizes are available at some home-improvement, hardware, and woodcrafter stores and some mail-order companies. In lieu of purchasing wood plugs, consider making your own.

Designed for use on drill presses only, Stanley *plug-cutter* bits do an excellent job of cutting out smooth wood plugs. These tools are available in different sizes to accommodate various needs. They cut like hole saws, but they have no pilot drills to give them stability; hence the required drill press.

Wood plugs do not have to be cut at any precise depth. In fact, it is best they remain a little too long. Plug ends that stick up past workpiece surfaces may be sanded down to match surrounding levels.

Drill bits operate best when they are sharp. Dull bits will tend to burn wood and will not make much of a dent in metal. Most saw-sharpening shops are able to sharpen bits. In addition, hardware and tool stores normally carry a small selection of guides designed to assist in bit sharpening. Check through the catalog pages of Harbor Freight Tools to locate specific tools designed for such work.

Saws & saw blades

IF DO-IT-YOURSELF homeowners had enough money, they might never need to use a saw. Money could be paid to lumber yards and cooperative home-improvement centers for cutting all wood to prescribed widths and lengths before delivery. This would negate any savings those do-it-yourselfers would have enjoyed had they done the wood cutting.

Every saw carries with it a potential for personal injury. Handsaws are perfectly capable of tearing through one's skin. Power saws never miss a beat when it comes to cutting off fingers, and their blades won't dull either. Therefore, always pay strict attention to every cutting task you undertake, wear safety goggles, maintain saw guards and shields, keep bystanders away from your work area, and understand all operating instructions before using any saw.

Numerous types of handsaws are available. Coping saws have skinny blades for intricate curved cuts; backsaws are rectangular with lots of teeth for accurate miter-cutting; keyhole saws have a pointed tip for close and confined work.

Handsaws

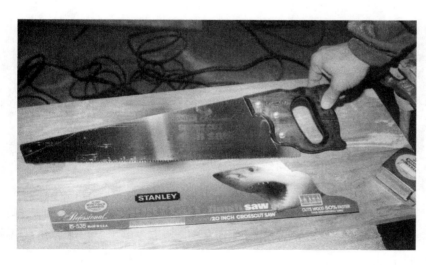

General *handsaws*, most frequently used to cut dimension lumber (2-by-4s, 2-by-6s, 4-by-4s, etc.), are available with 5½ teeth per inch for ripping and up to 12 teeth per inch for smooth crosscuts and some finish work. The more teeth a saw blade has per inch, the smoother it can cut. Keep your saw stored in its original protective sheath to protect teeth from accidental damage.

Hand-saws are very handy for cutting out that part of wood left uncut by power circular saws when notching out various pockets. Maintain your saw in a vertical position when nearing the end of such a cut to prevent cutting too far into the workpiece.

Young people just becoming acquainted with some home-improvement tools should first learn how to work accurately with hand tools before being introduced to power tools.

All sawing operations require that the work be firmly secured in position. Many handsaws are long, making them difficult to maneuver while workpieces are braced on short toolboxes or other things. Stanley's short-cut toolbox saw, made just for these occasions, is only 15 inches long; other handsaws range from 20 inches to 26 inches. The toolbox saw's length makes it easy to store in a normal toolbox and is also a good size for younger family members to work with.

Along with finishing handsaws, a Stanley nest of saws is a nice asset. Three different-purpose saw blades are interchangeable with a single handle.

After power had been disconnected to the electrical outlet, measurements were taken and marks made for wall cuts to accommodate moving the outlet to a higher position above a new workbench. Once a hole was made with a drill, a *compass saw* is used to cut out a small section of drywall. See top of next page.

Hacksaws are used for cutting metal, rigid plastic, and other hard materials. Blades have holes at each end that fit over small pegs. A wing-nut adjustment at the back end of blades or a knob on top of some hacksaw models is turned to place tension on blades, which keeps blades in place.

Stanley's high-tension hacksaw features a hollow top bar that is perfect for storing extra blades. Before installing a new blade, always look to see in which direction it is designed to cut. Printing on the side of new blades will include an arrow indicator or other instructions.

Power circular saws

Projects that include remodeling or new construction are well served by *power circular saws*. Used mainly on dimension lumber and plywood, these versatile tools serve a multitude of cutting purposes.

The Makita hypoid saw relies on hypoid gears to deliver maximum torque. It is different from other circular saws, which feature blades mounted directly to a motor shaft located on the right side of the motor.

The design of this hypoid saw allows right-handed users to see saw blades easily as they cut through pencil lines on wood. It is also easy to control and has an electric brake to slow down the saw blade once the operating trigger is released. A standard guide fits onto the front of this saw to help users make straight cuts. A wrench is provided to assist saw-blade changes.

Most circular saws are equipped with adjustments to regulate blade angles and depth. A depth control, located at the rear, consists of a long arm attached to the saw base secured by a lever.

Always be certain your circular saw has been disconnected from its power source before making adjustments. To lower a saw base and reduce cutting depth, simply loosen the control lever and move the base down. If you want an exact depth, use a piece of wood equal to the depth desired. Raise the saw-blade guard and rest the saw on that wood with the blade touching its side. Adjust the saw base down (or pull the saw motor up) until the base rests on top of the wood. Make sure the blade extends out from the base a distance equal to the wood's thickness. (Note: The safety guard is held open by the workpiece; it will slide back in place after the cut has been made.)

The Makita hypoid saw and most other circular saws are equipped with another adjustment located at the front of the base. This is used to control the blade's angle from 90 degrees to 45 degrees.

Again, unplug your saw before making any adjustments. To change a saw-blade angle, loosen the angle adjustment control lever and move the saw base until the desired degree indicator lines up with the main marker. Notice that there are two notches located at the front of the saw's base in line with the blade. One notch is used as a sight guide for 90-degree cuts, the other for 45-degree cuts.

Changing saw blades is a simple task as long as you read, understand, and follow operating instructions. If you do not have the saw's appropriate wrench, retrieve a hand wrench of the size needed to fit the nut securing the blade to the tool. The Makita hypoid saw has a button located at the front that is used to lock the saw's power shaft so that a wrench can unscrew the main blade bolt. That button is simply depressed and the blade slowly turned by hand until the blade and shaft lock in place. You'll feel the button push down farther when the locking notch lines up with it.

With the shaft and blade locked, twist the wrench in a clockwise direction to loosen it; it has left-hand threads. Pull out the bolt, retainer ring, and dull blade. When inserting a new blade, make sure blade teeth are pointed in the correct position. An arrow on the saw's guard shows that blades spin from the bottom toward the front; new saw blades have arrows too. Just remember that as a circular saw rests with the blade down (normal upright position), blade teeth on the very bottom should be pointing forward. This design ensures that saw blades cut into work from the bottom, forcing wood against saw bases.

Makita's 6¼-inch cordless circular saw is a powerful and very versatile tool. This saw works great for jobs on roofs, outbuildings located on open acreage, and anywhere else electrical power is not available. A large 10.8-volt battery supplies plenty of power to this saw. It comes with a battery, charger, carbide-tipped blade, socket wrench, hand wrench, and rip fence guide. The wooden storage box is optional.

Dimension lumber is no problem for the Makita cordless circular saw. It can quickly and easily cut through 2-by-4, 2-by-6, and other lumber of comparable thicknesses. The unit, lightweight and maneuverable, is equipped with adjustments for blade depth and angle. Do not underestimate the power, torque, and cutting abilities of this saw. It is every bit as good as one with an electrical cord. (Note: The safety guard in this illustration is held open by the workpiece; it will slide back in place after the cut has been made.)

Another very impressive battery-powered circular saw is Makita's 3⅜-inch cordless saw. Designed for trim work, this unit creates an unbelievable torque. Give this tool all the respect you have for other power saws.

To change saw blades on the Makita 3⅜-inch cordless saw, use its hex key wrench, which rests in the handy pocket located near the top front of the motor head. This wrench is also used for changing the blade depth and angle. An assortment of saw blades is available for this unit. Although not really designed for cutting plywood, this saw goes through ¾-inch shop-grade plywood as easily as any other.

Always position circular saws so that the main body rests on the part that will remain secured and not the part that is being cut off. This is a fundamental safety and precision-cutting concern.

Be sure to maintain a steady grip on this saw. Should its slim blade bind in any way, torque will force the tool right out of its work. Wear safety goggles and make certain the board you are cutting is completely secured in position; Quick-Grip bar clamps are perfect for these operations.

Makita's small cordless circular saw works great for normally awkward tasks like trimming out wood siding for the installation of new doors and windows. Because it is lightweight and cordless, this tool makes those kinds of jobs safer. Another advantage to the size of this tool is its ability to cut close to nearby obstructions—for example, cutting out countertop sections for sink installations where backsplashes are already in place. Countertops must be cut close to backsplashes and regular power-saw bases are generally too wide for those spaces.

Circular saws are designed to make straight cuts. They cannot be expected to cut intricate curves and circles. However, *reciprocating saws* employ a completely different set of saw blades designed for all kinds of interesting maneuvers.

On the Makita Recipro saw, the slim straight blade on this tool goes in and out at a very rapid speed to cut through a variety of materials, determined by the type of blade used. It can cut

Reciprocating saws

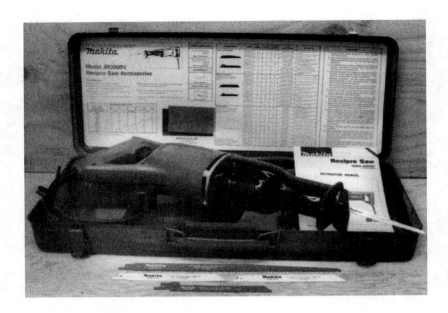

through metal, plastic, pipe, wood, and just about anything else—as long as the appropriate blade is attached. The case that comes with the Makita Recipro saw includes an informative label that describes this tool's abilities and the functions of various blade types.

To prolong the life of Recipro saw blades, adjust the tool's shoe to a fully extended position after the insertion of a new blade. Once the end of the blade becomes dull, simply adjust that shoe back toward the tool. The rear portion of the blade will still be like new. The shoe may also be adjusted for various cutting endeavors. You may find that certain objects on a structure have an obstruction close behind. Adjust the tool's shoe so that the blade extends only far enough for cutting needs. Likewise, for jobs requiring long cuts, reposition the shoe closer to the tool body.

This saw is indispensable for home remodeling work. Tearing apart existing home components to make way for new additions will call for numerous wall, stud, and other framing cuts on old structural members. Usually, circular saws will be too big for these jobs. The maneuverability of this Recipro saw, along with its variety of blades is a dream come true for home remodelers.

Makita also offers a powerful cordless Recipro saw. As part of the 9.6-volt system, the battery for this unit is compatible with lots of other cordless tools. Once the battery becomes discharged, put it in the charger, retrieve a fresh battery from the idle 3⅜-inch cordless saw, and keep working.

Like its big brother, this saw can use an assortment of blades. A hex key is stored in a handy pocket and used for changing blades. The dual safety-trigger assembly requires that both triggers be activated before the tool turns on to prevent accidental activation. Once again, you must respect the power of this cordless tool. Wear safety goggles and thoroughly read and comprehend all operating instructions.

Walls are normally framed with base mudsills where doorways are planned. This length of wood is left in place while framing as a means to add strength to walls before they are completely nailed in place. Afterward, that section of mudsill must be removed. A Recipro saw is perfect for this chore. Always use caution when cutting close to floors. Balance the tool on its shoe so that the blade does not come in contact with the floor. Should a small amount of wood still remain at the base of such a cut, use a hand chisel to chip it away after knocking the piece of wood out of the space.

Because Recipro saws are commonly used to cut away material from existing walls during remodeling activities, users must be keenly aware of obstacles behind wall surfaces. All electrical power should be turned off to outlets and switches near cutting areas to prevent electrocution should a saw blade come in contact with an electrical wire. Likewise, should a *blind cut* be planned near water pipes, plan to have a plumber drain and cap pipes before cutting begins.

Jigsaws Geared more toward hobbyist and fine finished craftsmanship work, *jigsaws* employ a concept similar to that of reciprocating saws. The blades for these tools reciprocate back and forth, but from the bottom of their host tools as opposed to the nose of Recipro saws.

The Makita cordless jigsaw, also part of the 9.6-volt system, has the ability to share batteries with the 3⅜-inch saw, ⅜-inch driver-drill, cordless Recipro saw, and other compatible cordless tools. This unit may be used to cut out patterns in plywood, some dimension lumber, plastic, and numerous other materials as long as the appropriate blade is installed. Its battery will keep the tool cutting through 39 feet of ½-inch wood.

You must read blade information before attempting to cut anything. Blades are designed for a number of different applications. Inappropriately employed, blades could damage work, shatter, or cause other problems.

Optional guides are available for the Makita cordless jigsaw. Jigsaws have bases that can be adjusted to accommodate angled cuts. The blade operates normally, but the angle of the base causes the entire unit to ride on top of the workpiece at the desired angle. A hex key is kept in a handy pocket for use during blade changes and bevel adjustments. To change cutting angles, simply loosen a hex-head screw located in the middle of the saw shoe, then rotate the shoe to the degree desired. Be sure to tighten the shoe's hex screw once it has been properly adjusted.

For more power in cutting through thicker materials and for more prolonged use, consider the Makita electronic jigsaw.

It has an electronic speed control that maintains a constant speed regardless of load for maximum production. An orbital blade option offers three positions for wood and one nonorbital for metal. This is a variable-speed model with six-stage speed settings for precise cutting. The shoe is adjustable for up to 45-degree cutting right or left.

It comes with two blades, hex wrench, and steel carrying case. As with the cordless jigsaw, you must understand that the type of blade used with this tool is of paramount concern. The right blade must be used for the right job. Optional guides are available for this electronic jigsaw, including one designed for circle cutting.

Hobbyists frequently require cutting tools that offer a means for maximum work control. Although a great deal of this type of work can be accomplished with jigsaws, many prefer to use a tool where workpieces are moved around a stationary cutter for decorative trim pieces on fascia boards for older homes, interior decor arrangements, and so on.

This scroll saw from Harbor Freight Tools features a cast-iron base to support work that is moved about while being cut by a blade that remains fixed in one location. Rocker arms help to keep work secured. Combined with a constant-tension feature and pivoting blade suspension, blade breakage is held at a minimum while providing consistent cuts. This saw will handle up to 2-inch-thick material, and the table will tilt to accommodate bevel cuts. For precision cutting where patterns, curves, and odd shapes are required, consider this 16-inch benchtop scroll saw from Harbor Freight Tools.

Harbor Freight Tools

Table saws   The Makita 10-inch table saw is capable of cutting wood up to 3³⁄₁₆ inches thick at 90 degrees and 2½ inches at 45 degrees. Used mainly for cabinetmaking and finish-carpentry operations,

table saws provide a means to achieve precision cuts for all sorts of woodworking and home-improvement endeavors.

Using the sliding miter table, boards can be crosscut precisely at 90 degrees or any other angle. The blade is adjustable up and down to accommodate thick and thin materials. It is best to adjust table-saw blades to a maximum point where only the top teeth of the blade extend past the top of work. Having too much of the blade stick up is dangerous and unnecessary.

The Makita table saw rip-fence attachment is designed for assisting in cuts made along wood grains; down the length of 2-by-4s, plywood, and so on. Position the rip fence according to the distance between its inside face and the outer tips of saw blades. Be certain your Makita table saw is unplugged and disconnected from its power supply before making adjustments.

The sliding miter table on Makita's 10-inch table saw is equipped with an adjustable arm. The arm can be rotated and secured from 90 degrees to 45 degrees. This assists with angled crosscutting endeavors. A small block of wood is secured at the end of this arm and used as a blade guide. After being secured in the miter adjustment arm, the block of wood is run through the saw blade. Once that occurs, users know exactly where cuts will be made, as determined by the end of that wood block.

This table saw also features a handy pocket for the storage of blade-changing tools and operating instructions. Please note the warning sticker next to the storage pocket. Many tool manufacturers such as Makita and Stanley have gone out of their way to ensure that appropriate safety warnings are posted on their tools and equipment. Operators are urged again and again to abide by safety recommendations to avoid personal injury. You are once again reminded to read, comprehend, and follow all operating instructions for all tools and equipment.

When using powerful cutting tools, plan ahead to ensure safe operations. Never position yourself in line with saw blades, and always be alert to every step you make and the locations of your hands and fingers. Enlist the use of helpers while working with large pieces of wood.

Miter saws

Home-improvement endeavors frequently require boards to be cut at various angles. Objectives like these can be accomplished with hand and power saws as long as operators measure and mark precisely and operate saws with impeccable accuracy. Another means of achieving accurate 90-degree and angled cuts is *miter saws*.

Makita's 10-inch slide compound saw is capable of cutting wood at any angle. This saw can cut boards at two angles with just one cut, referred to as a *compound cut*. Do-it-yourself remodelers faced with stick-framing new roofs over existing roofs that extend at a perpendicular angle will need to make numerous compound angle cuts to accommodate rafter ends.

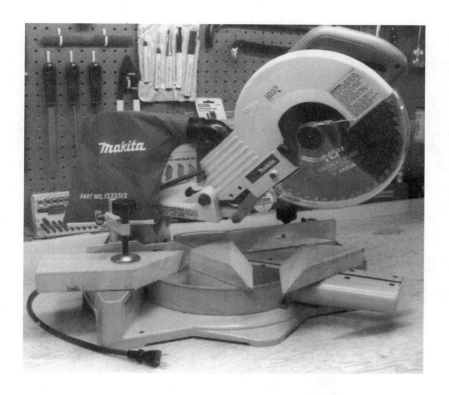

Miter saws, also commonly referred to as *chop saws*, are great work savers when it comes to interior finish work and the installation of base, window, door, and other molding pieces. These saws are easily and quickly rotated to any angle. Once locked in place, all cuts will be made identically. Read the operating instructions before putting this quality saw to work.

In addition to compound cuts, Makita's slide compound saw is able to cut boards up to 12 inches wide. Once a wide piece of material is positioned and then secured with a hold-down mechanism and with the machine in the *off* position, pull the saw toward you as far as it will come. With safety goggles on, pull the operating trigger and slowly push the blade into the work. Then maneuver the saw toward the back until your cut is complete.

An assortment of saw blades capable of numerous cutting applications is available for this saw—for example, an aluminum cutting blade and a long-lasting carbide-tipped blade. A socket wrench required for blade changes is stored in a handy pocket located at the rear of the unit. Don't forget to empty the sawdust bag on a regular basis.

Another type of miter saw is designed for cutting metal pipe, round and square tubing, bars, and other heavy-duty metal components.

The Makita 16-inch cut-off saw is equipped with an abrasive wheel that relies on friction to cut metals. Therefore, be prepared for a lot of hot sparks that will fly out of the blade's protective guard. Make sure a noncombustible plate is located behind the saw to prevent spark damage, or use this saw on a concrete floor with plenty of open space behind it.

Due to the effects of metal cutting, you must wear full face protection. In addition, you should seriously consider a respirator to avoid breathing in fumes created by this type of friction cutting.

The quick-release vise provided with Makita's cut-off saw is adjustable to 45 degrees. A socket wrench provided with the unit is used to loosen bolts that secure this vise to the work base. For wide workpieces, another set of bolt holes is provided for moving the vise's backing plate farther toward the rear.

For storage, a chain is used to secure the saw's cutting head in a closed position so that it will fit into cabinet spaces. A depth-control arm must be adjusted appropriately to prevent the abrasive wheel from cutting too deep into a workbench top or other supporting surface.

Some reference has already been made about different types of saw blades and their specific uses. The following is a closer look at some circular saw blades and their unique characteristics.

Saw blades

Fundamentally, *rip* refers to cutting along wood grains. *Crosscut* means cutting across the grain. *Combination* blades are designed to cut in both rip and crosscut patterns.

The difference in saw blades, other than diameter, is their tooth configuration. In essence, the more teeth a blade has, the smoother it will cut. Blades spaced far apart will chew through wood leaving behind large splintered edges.

Ripping through wood is easier on saws. Not as many teeth are needed because wood tends naturally to come apart between grains; note how easily wood splits along its grain if you attempt to drive a large nail into it. On the other hand, cutting across grain requires more teeth because saws have to dig through each grain and actually cut fibers as opposed to running along their length. Chisel-tooth blades combine the best of both rip and crosscut configurations to offer a manageable means of ripping and crosscutting with a minimum of splintered edges.

Carbide-tipped blades are designed to last for a long time. The carbide-tip sections attached to blade teeth are extremely hard, so hard that ordinary sharpening wheels will hardly make a dent in them. Carbide-tipped blades cost more than regular blades but last a great deal longer. Cutting through an occasional staple or small nail will not dull these blades nearly as fast as others. The cost to sharpen carbide-tipped blades will be more than that for ordinary blades because sharpening shops must maintain a special grinding-wheel system just for them.

The printing applied to most saw blades normally includes warnings and recommendations about personal safety, the blade's diameter size, its tooth configuration, and an arrow indicating in which direction it is designed to rotate.

Many 7¼-inch circular saw blades are equipped with *knockouts*. This means that blades can be used on saws with round arbors (designated by the round hole in the middle) as well as saws that require the special arbor fitting that corresponds to the outline around such holes. The metal inside the outline on those blades is knocked out and discarded to facilitate installation on such saws.

Different blade styles are also available for the Makita 3⅜-inch cordless saw—a carbide-tipped blade, a plywood blade, and an all-purpose trim blade. The plywood and trim blades are very thin and require users to make very straight cuts to prevent blades from binding. Holes in the blades are provided as a means for the saw's locking mechanism to secure them and the saw shaft from turning while the hex-key retaining screw is loosened and tightened.

Have you ever wondered how deep grooves are sawn into the sides of shelf units for the insertion of long metal brackets that support small hooks upon which shelves are placed? Chances are, they were sawn with the use of a table-saw *dado*. A dado system involves the use of a number of cutting blades to cut grooves in wood at various widths.

The Makita 6-inch dado head set includes two outside cutters with a 6-inch diameter and ⅛-inch thickness, four inside cutters at ⅛ inch thick, one inside cutter at 1/16 inch thick, and three rings. Per instructions, these dado assemblies can be mixed and matched to achieve a number of different-width dado cuts (across grain) or grooves (with grain). In addition to the dado system, you will need to insert an optional table-saw insert to accommodate the thickness of these blades.

Band saws use blades that are completely different from any other. Band-saw blades are flexible strips of thin metal manufactured in a complete circle. They spin around in a continuous circle. A variety of tooth configurations are available for cutting various materials and thicknesses. In essence, band saws are similar to scroll saws; scroll-saw blades are single straight strips and band-saw blades are continuous strips.

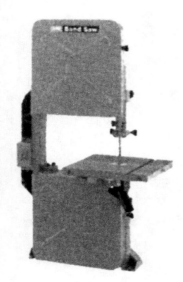

This Makita band saw incorporates a blade that makes a complete vertical loop around the machine. Instead of relying upon reciprocating blade action, band-saw blades continue in the same cutting direction at all times. This makes it possible for users to cut thick slabs of wood in almost any pattern. Thinner blades are used for curved cuts; wider blades work best for cuts in extra-thick workpieces. Operating directions illustrate how to accomplish angle, straight, curved, and special cuts.

Saws are wonderful tools. They will cut through numerous materials perfectly as long as the operator controls their movements and operations effectively. Whenever operating a saw, always go the extra mile to ensure safe operation according to the manufacturer's recommendations. Accidents with powerful saws are unforgiving. Do not lose sight of the reasons you are undertaking home-improvement tasks—to save money and gain the personal satisfaction of knowing that you did it yourself. Those commendable reasons will be long forgotten if you end up in a hospital.

Routers, trimmers, & shapers

CABINET and cupboard doors are frequently outfitted with *routed* or shaped edges. Newer designs that feature squared-off edges for such assemblies are most often faced with a laminate material. Laminates must have their edges trimmed to fit flush and be smooth.

In workshops and places where dust may be a problem, the inside edges of cabinet and cupboard doors should be shaped so that part of them fits inside their openings. The type of cut employed for such occasions is called a *rabbet*.

Routers, trimmers, and shapers employ specific bits that are capable of accomplishing any number of wood-shaping endeavors. In a most general way, routers and their bits are maneuvered by hand to make certain kinds of grooves or decorative edges on wood. Shapers, in a sense, are extra-large stationary routers. Like scroll saws, work is brought to shapers; the tool cannot be moved. Trimmers are most widely used for trimming excess material from countertop edges, although they can also be used with templates to perform routerlike work.

Routers, trimmers, & shapers 85

Routers

Routers are basically big motors outfitted with a high-speed spindle at their base into which router bits are secured.

Wrenches are needed to hold spindle shafts while collars are loosened for the insertion and removal of bits. Guides, like the straight guide attached to this Makita plunge router, are secured to router bases and used to help operators maintain control of tools so that they go in the direction desired.

Always be certain routers have been disconnected from their power supply before attempting to adjust them or change bits. Router bits spin at exceptionally high speeds and could cause very serious injuries.

The powerful Makita 1⅜ horsepower (HP) router comes with a ½-inch *collet*, which means that bits must have ½-inch shanks to be used on this machine. Large ½-inch shank bits are designed for heavy-duty and prolonged work. Many router bits are manufactured with ¼-inch shanks. To use smaller shank bits, this tool comes with a ¼-inch collet sleeve.

To adjust router-bit depth of cut, a router motor is adjusted up or down from its base. Most models, like this Makita 1⅜ HP router, feature a locking knob and twisting ring.

The frame that supports the router motor is firmly attached to the unit's base. Once the locking knob has been loosened, rotation of a threaded twist ring around the motor will cause the motor to go up or down, moving the router bit up or down along with it. Once a desired depth is established, the locking knob is tightened, and the bit will cut at the same depth until adjusted again.

A variation from this kind of twist-ring depth adjustment is found on *plunge routers*. These tools are capable of being pushed down into work from a sitting position. An example of where such a plunge is useful is a groove to be cut in the middle of a board, the groove extending no closer than 6 inches from the edge. How does one get the groove started in the middle of a board?

After making the proper adjustments to the Makita 1¼ HP plunge router, per operating instructions, it can be placed upright on top of the workpiece. Its appropriate handle is loosened to allow the machine to be pushed down into the work.

Used in conjunction with a guide, this router can now be maneuvered down the length of a board to make the desired

groove. Once it reaches the end of the groove, it is turned off and raised back to its upright position.

Guides are very important router accessories. Without them, users would have a difficult time controlling their movement when using certain kinds of bits.

Here, a *straight guide* has been secured to the Makita 1⅜ HP router to keep the machine going straight along the side of a workbench. This guide can be adjusted in or out. Along with straight guides, users can select from a number of templates for making letters, scrolls, and other designs. A *template guide* is attached to the router base for use with templates. In addition, some work along wood edges may be accomplished with special bits that are equipped with a roller. This roller prevents bits from cutting into work too deeply and helps keep the router on course.

Whenever working with routers, always have a piece of scrapwood available for running test cuts. Such cuts allow operators to measure actual results and make fine-tuning adjustments before routing on workpieces.

Making test cuts is very important when working with guides to make grooves on plywood sheets that will be used as shelf supports. If one side of the shelf support groove ends up higher than the other, shelves will sit cockeyed, look awkward, and be inefficient.

Refer to your router's operating instructions to ensure that you operate this tool in the correct direction. This helps to keep guides firmly pulled into work and greatly assists in making clean cuts.

When making cabinets and cupboards that require numerous grooves, plan to measure your work periodically to ensure accurate cutting results. Check tightening knobs and levers on your router too.

Guides that attach to router bases have a limited range. For router work required in the middle of long wide boards or sheets of plywood, consider using a long *all-purpose guide*.

This all-purpose guide from Harbor Freight Tools is secured to plywood with Quick-Grip bar clamps. The Makita plunge router was adjusted for depth, then locked in place for a complete groove cut. After marking the location where the groove was to be cut, measurements for the placement of this guide took into account the distance from the router's base side that would run against it to the near edge of the router bit. Had that extra distance not been accounted for, the groove would have been cut a few inches from where it was intended to be.

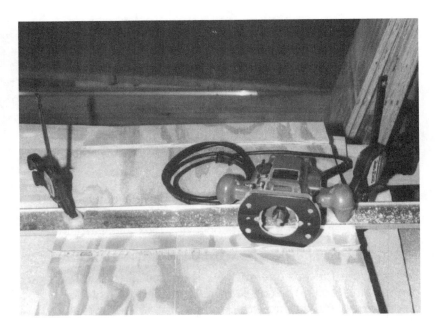

Router bits

The number of router bits available is impressive. Various shapes and sizes are capable of a wide assortment of designs. Since it is sometimes difficult to determine the kinds of cuts router bits are made for, manufacturers generally include an illustration on bit packages that shows an example.

Makita router bits come in heavy plastic bags that are inscribed with illustrations depicting the type of cut each bit is designed to accomplish. You are encouraged to store bits in their bags so that you can always tell at a glance which bits will cut which designs. These bags also help to protect bits from dust and moisture.

Although router bits may be purchased individually, you may discover that better overall bargains are found with sets.

The Makita nine-piece deluxe carbide-tipped router-bit set includes nine very popular router bits. The case includes a clear window that slides out for bit retrieval and a swivel mounting board that makes getting bits in and out quite easy. As with new self-feed drilling bits, these bits are covered at the factory with a thick waxlike covering as protection.

Although properly equipped trimmers are capable of accomplishing some light router-type work, they are really geared toward tasks involving trim work.

Trimmers

Bits designed for use with tools like the Makita cordless trimmer look very much like high-speed twist-drill bits, but trimmer bits include cutting blades at their tips and their flutes have sharp edges to cut along with tips.

Equipped with appropriate guides, Makita trimmers are capable of cutting circles, grooves, bevels, and other shapes. Cutting bevel edges around workpiece edges requires a special trimmer guide that causes the tool to tilt at a 45-degree angle so that the tip can cut what is needed. This guide's base also helps to control the trimmers to keep it on course along table edges, countertop edges, and the like.

Other guides rely on a bottom roller to keep trimmer cutters properly adjusted. This is important while working along the edges of workpieces to ensure against gouges or missed sections.

One of the most popular jobs for trimmers is the removal of extra laminate material that extends over the edges of countertops. Laminates for countertops are not cut to specific shapes or sizes and then glued in place. Rather, large sheets are brought to work sites and then cut to shape. Extra material is allowed to hang over the edges on purpose. Once material is secured in place and glue set, the edges are trimmed so they match up perfectly with countertop faces.

Trimmers are lightweight tools with very high RPM ratings. The Makita ½-HP trimmer, for example has a 28,000-RPM 3.3-amp hi-tech motor. The relatively high speeds these tools put out help their trimmer bits do an excellent job of trimming materials quickly and smoothly.

If you mounted your router on a router table, you would essentially have a small *shaper*. Router tables are set up so that routers can be securely mounted to their undersides. Routers are set in an upside-down position so that their bits stick

Shapers

straight up through a hole in the middle of the table. For all practical purposes, shapers are extra-heavy-duty routers mounted on special worktables.

Big motors power shaper machines to give the ability to cut thick materials. In addition, many special *shaper cutters* are multifaceted; they can make two or more cuts on work with just one pass.

Adjustments to shaper fences and cutters will determine what kinds of cuts are achieved. Plan to have scrap lumber available for making test cuts.

A closer view of this shaper shows that a series of handles and knobs are used to adjust the fences (they are separate) and the safety hold-down arms. A clear cutter head guard has been removed to show what the cutter head looks like. The operating spindle that spins the cutter head is adjusted up and down by controls located under the table. Obtaining satisfactory results with shapers requires users to understand and follow all operating instructions.

Decorative posts adorned with variously shaped grooves that support porch roofs, stair railings, and other upright objects were probably shaped on a *wood lathe*. More fine woodworking machines than home-improvement tools, lathes are designed to spin long pieces of wood in a horizontal position while an operator uses *lathe knives* to cut grooves in the stock. Lathe knives are supported by a *tool rest*. Users gently push knives into wood to effect deeper cuts. Various knife styles allow different shapes in the wood stock.

On the left side of this wood-turning lathe from Harbor Freight Tools is the headstock (motor); it is responsible for spinning wood at prescribed speeds. To the far right is the tailstock, which secures the opposite end of the workpiece. In the middle is the tool rest, which slides left and right to accommodate knife maneuvering.

Many tools and accessories are designed to shape wood accurately and smoothly, trim laminates, and accomplish similar tasks. Each tool and accessory will do an excellent job as long as the person operating it has set up the adjustments correctly, uses the items as intended, and pays strict attention to the work at hand.

Always read, understand, and follow operating instructions. Wear safety goggles; keep long hair pinned up or under a hat; and wear close-fitting clothing. Loose sleeves, unbuttoned shirts, long hair, and the like can easily be snagged and rapidly drawn in by fast-turning tools.

CHAPTER 8

Planes, planers, & jointers

ALTHOUGH many hand and power tools are capable of cutting boards straight and smooth, the perfection provided by planes, planers, and jointers is required for numerous *finishing* tasks—making cabinet and cupboard faces, fitting doors, smoothing and finishing interior window trim, and so on.

Planes are hand tools equipped with thick blades that peel away small layers of wood with each pass. *Hand power planers* are in the same category as power drills and circular saws, their purpose being to smooth and level the edges of wood boards. Planers are large machines designed to smooth and level wide faces of boards.

Jointers are used to smooth and flatten board edges perfectly straight and even. Their operation is similar to hand power planers except that work is brought to them.

Hand planes

More than a dozen hand planes are available through the *Stanley Tools Full Line Catalog* in different cutter-blade sizes, blade-angle positions, bottom shoe lengths, and handle designs.

The Stanley professional bench plane is a handsome and sturdy tool. Its mouth opening is adjustable for coarse or fine work. A sharp blade adjusted correctly according to directions will peel away long strips of wood with each pass. This tool works well to smooth and level rough wood edges.

The blade cutters on hand planes do not need to be adjusted too far out from their bases. Those that do will be difficult or impossible to maneuver because they are trying to cut much too deep. Planes need only to peel away small layers of wood with each pass.

Finish-carpentry tasks generally do not involve removing large amounts of wood. Rather, quality work commonly relies upon careful use of planes and sandpaper to make fine, smooth, and even finishes.

Another type of hand plane available to professionals and do-it-yourselfers is called a *rabbet plane*. The Stanley rabbet plane features adjustable guides that allow users to make rabbet cuts. Rabbets can be put on cabinet doors to help keep dust out, planks for lap joints, and other wood items. This tool has two seats for the cutter; one for regular work and another for *bullnose* operations—working close to obstructions like backsplashes, walls, moldings, and the like.

Before purchasing the first hand plane you see, seriously consider what types of finishing projects are in front of you. Will you be doing a lot of bullnose or rabbeting work by hand? Or would a small *block plane* be better for a few minor planing jobs?

Power hand planes

Adjusted correctly according to operating instructions and with sharp blades, *power hand planes* are capable of peeling away a lot of wood in a hurry. Workpieces must be secured well before work begins.

The Makita 3¼-inch planer can plane door edges in just seconds. An extra-long electrical service cord allows users plenty of working room while smoothing or cutting down edges on lengthy doors, boards, or other units. Be sure to wear safety goggles and avoid bulky clothing that could get caught up in the planer blades.

The Makita 3¼-inch planer features two cutting blades attached to a shaft that spins around at speeds up to 16,000 RPM. The front shoe on this planer is adjusted up or down to determine cutting depth.

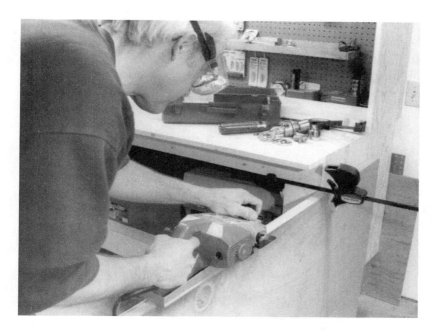

Always make sure your planer is unplugged when making adjustments or changing cutter blades. Next to the planer is its guide. This unit is also adjustable to conform to workpiece widths. Generally, longer shoes on planers make them easier to maneuver and control.

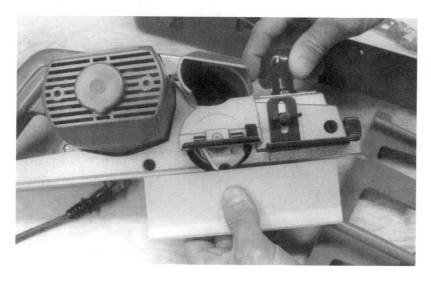

Notice that the front shoe on this Makita planer is adjusted much higher than the back one and that the cutter blade is adjusted in perfect balance with the back shoe. Since planers are designed to start their work at the end of a board, you can see that blades will cut at a depth in proportion to the height of the front shoe; back shoes remain stationary and are not adjustable.

If a board has a knothole or deep gouge in the middle of its edge, a long front shoe will span the blemish, allowing cutters to remove wood material around it. As passes continue, enough material will have been removed so that the entire edge of the board will soon be equal to the level at the bottom of the knothole. In other words, you will have planed the board edge to a perfectly flat surface by removing the knothole through planing the rest of the board's edge to a level past the bottom of that blemish.

Jointers

An easy way to understand the purpose of *jointers* is to imagine a hand power planer secured upside down on a worktable. This piece of equipment is a Makita 12½-inch planer-jointer. Two tools in one, the unit features a 6⅛-inch jointer on one side with a wide planer in the middle. Planers will be covered later in this chapter.

Rubber-based *push blocks* (paddles) are used to slide small pieces over the jointer blades. A quarter-round spring-loaded guard covers the cutting blades not engaged in planing wood. The tool's power cord is secured to an extension cord of equal size, tied in a loose square knot at the plug connection and positioned out of the way of jointing operations.

With the Makita planer-jointer unplugged and the jointer's safety guard pulled away, you can see a cutting blade. Wood is always fed over this tool's cutting blades from right to left. Therefore, the right side of the worktable is adjusted up or down to determine cutting depths. The fence (upright backing plate) is adjustable from front to back to accommodate different wood width sizes. Working on thin pieces of wood, the fence is moved forward, and a small safety lid in back is then closed over that portion of the cutter opening not involved in the operation.

With the safety guard completely removed and the machine unplugged from its power supply, you can see how lowering the front of the worktable will determine cutting depth.

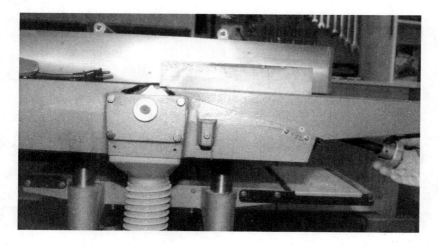

Notice the adjustment wheel at the far right and a cutting-depth indicator just in front of it. The operation is simple; turning the wheel activates a large screw mechanism to push or pull that part of the table up or down along its angled base. The round knob located at the end of the cutter assembly is used to turn the cutters by hand for positioning when replacing or adjusting blades. The corrugated hose extending down from the bottom of the jointer is part of the Makita dust-collector system.

The cutting blades on this Makita jointer are secured to their power shaft by four heavy-duty bolts. Leveling devices included with the machine are used to adjust blades to a perfect working height. Jointer blades can be sharpened many times. As they become shorter because of honing or grinding, their position can be pushed a bit forward on their power shaft through adjustments made possible by large slotted bolt-hole openings. Follow operating instructions carefully when changing or adjusting blades. These items must be replaced perfectly, or your work will not be flat and true.

Jointing

The term *jointing* refers to operations to make the sides of boards perfectly flat, straight, and even. Each time you run a board through the jointer, a little material will be taken off.

To join boards side-to-side forming a perfect joint, the sides must be smoothed and flattened so that they match as one—hence the purpose of jointers. Although wood glue works very well to secure wood pieces together tightly, there are times when joints must be reinforced. This is accomplished through *dovetails*, *tongue-and-groove*, *tenon-and-mortise*, or other jointing techniques.

A quick and simple means of creating strong wood joints is *biscuits*—small football-shaped pieces of wood inserted and glued halfway into one board and halfway into another. The Freud joiner system includes a joiner machine, splines (biscuits), and a glue-applicator unit. Here the Freud joiner machine has been used to make cuts in board sides to accommodate the insertion of splines.

The locations where cuts are made must line up on each board that will mate with another. To ensure that, operators position boards together as they want them to be once the job is complete. In that position, pencil lines are made across them to designate cut sites. These lines will be removed later when the finished product is fed through the planer or sanded smooth.

It is also wise to number each board so that its original position can be easily established after cutting has been completed.

Splines, also referred to by many as biscuits or *wood wafers*, are available in different sizes. Size 0 is quite small, followed by 10 and 20. Smaller pieces to be joined together require only small splines. Bigger pieces need bigger splines. It is that easy. Of course, if you want a particular joint to be extra strong for some reason, there is no problem with inserting large splines as long as wood pieces are big enough to accommodate them.

The pencil lines on wood pieces serve the critical purpose of designating where cuts are to be made. To make these cuts effectively, simply line up the center mark on a clearly visible spot on the joiner machine with the board marks.

According to the joiner machine's operating instructions, you should have adjusted the tool's depth and height before attempting any cuts. To ensure that your adjustments are accurate, make sample cuts on a piece of scrapwood and measure. The Freud joiner machine has a front fence that is adjusted up and down according to the thickness of workpieces. In addition, the fence can be used at a 45-degree angle for special joinery operations.

Once all cuts have been made, it is time to glue the biscuits and boards together. Freud has introduced a great gluing system that includes a unique applicator and reservoir. The glue applicator features a spout that is thin and wide, perfect for fitting into biscuit cuts. Use it to apply glue inside cuts and over biscuits. Spread glue over the surface of board edges too.

When you have completed a gluing section, simply place the applicator into the reservoir for handy storage. The reservoir has a large sponge inside saturated with water to a corresponding mark on the reservoir's side. While working with the Freud gluing system, the applicator can be placed inside the

reservoir where its tip will remain in constant contact with water so that the glue will not dry and harden. When you have completed all of your biscuit operations, clean the tip thoroughly with water, replace it on the bottle, and snap on its protective cover, conveniently attached to it with a plastic chain.

Wood that has been glued together must be held secure with clamps until glue has had an opportunity to dry completely and set. Quick-Grip bar clamps from American Tool Companies are handy and reliable. As you tighten clamps, be sure wood pieces are lined up as you want them. Although biscuits will add great strength to joints, they are not initially tight. Glue will cause biscuits to swell with time, but early on, as boards are clamped together, you may have to push and pull on them so that their wide faces match one another more smoothly.

Planers (planing machines)

Planers use the same kinds of cutter blades as hand power planers and jointers but are generally much longer. Power hand planers and jointers are designed to plane wood edges. Planers are geared toward planing wide faces.

Next to the on-off mechanism on this Makita planer-jointer, a rule gauge designates how thick wood will be when it exits the machine. The small pointer gauge in the center of the planer indicates how deep the cut will be. Note that the deepest cut possible is ⅛ inch. You can accomplish deeper cuts by simply running workpieces through numerous times.

Like other planing blades, those for this machine can be sharpened. Leveling devices included with the Makita planer-jointer assist operators in positioning blades accurately. Be certain to unplug planers before attempting adjustments or blade replacements, and follow instructions completely.

The Makita planer-jointer comes with a set of instructions, servicing hand tools, levelers, cutter-blade sharpening guides, and push blocks. Take advantage of these accessories whenever servicing the machine or adjusting parts. Store these items in the convenient storage box and keep it in a handy location for quick retrieval.

As mentioned, you must ensure that machines are unplugged from their power supply before attempting any adjustment, blade change, or service work. To lock the shafts for both the planer and jointer on this Makita machine, simply operate the locking lever located under the planer's protective metal hood.

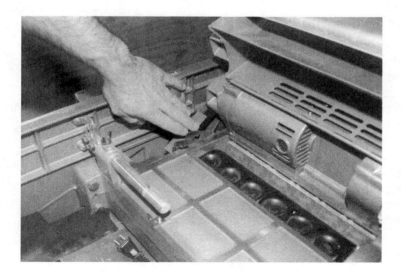

This locking feature is a real asset for loosening and removing dull planer or jointer blades. Before locking the shaft, though, use the knurled knob located near the jointer to turn the power shaft until blade-securing bolts are plainly in sight and in an accessible position.

Concrete planers

Some projects may call for new concrete applications to cover trenches that had to be dug through concrete floors for the installation of plumbing or drainpipe. Once in a while, new concrete sections poured to fill trenches result in uneven finishes, rough edges, or seams that do not quite match the surrounding surface. Many of those jobs can be smoothed out and repaired with help from a *concrete planer*.

Makita's concrete planer employs a dry-cutting diamond wheel for planing without water. The tool's front roller adjusts to accommodate depths. In addition, users can adjust the concrete planer's shoe for extra-smooth results. A rubber collar fitted over the diamond cutting wheel helps to control planing dust and guide it toward the dustbag.

Even with a dust-control collar and bag, expect this powerful machine to kick up quite a bit of concrete dust. Along with personal safety equipment, plan to close doors and seal gaps with tape to prevent clouds of concrete dust from infiltrating your home. When smoothing concrete walls or other installations outdoors, be sure nearby windows are closed.

Wear a quality respirator and safety goggles whenever using a concrete planer. The power behind this machine is very impressive; it knocks down concrete ridges in just seconds. Adjust the machine to plane just a minimal amount of concrete on initial exercises. Set too deep, this fast-working concrete planer will cause gouges and ridges. Start shallow and graduate as needed to maintain complete control of the overall planing operation.

A great deal of satisfaction is gained from successfully planing a piece of wood or concrete to perfection. Family members and friends will admire your work and wonder how you accomplished it. Some of the tools described in this chapter require a bit of practice on scrap material before attempting work on expensive pieces of wood. After reading and fully comprehending all operating instructions, plan to spend time planing and jointing with extra materials to get a feel for how these tools and machines operate.

Once again, pay strict attention to all safety and operating recommendations. Companies that make these tools have spent untold hours researching and developing the most efficient means for using them safely and effectively. Take full advantage of their advice.

CHAPTER 9

Sanders & sandpaper

AFTER CUTTING, drilling, routing, planing, jointing, and mounting cabinets, counters, and so on, a final step is necessary before staining or painting. That step involves careful sanding to ensure that all surfaces, joints, and edges are perfectly smooth to enhance overall luster and beauty when pieces are stained or painted.

Although you may consider tackling some small or intricate sanding tasks by hand, a number of power *sanders* are available that can make lots of sanding jobs much easier. *Large belt sanders*, like the Makita model at far left, work fast to smooth rough surfaces. Lighter-weight *finishing sanders*, like the Makita models in the middle, perform their jobs with less vigor than belt sanders and are much gentler on surfaces to produce exceptionally smooth final sanding results.

Some sanding tasks, like drywall finishing, must be done by hand using rigid *sanding boards* to guarantee flat results.

Using a belt sander or other power model on soft and easily blemished drywall is not recommended. These powerful tools will sand much too deep so quickly that drywall textures could

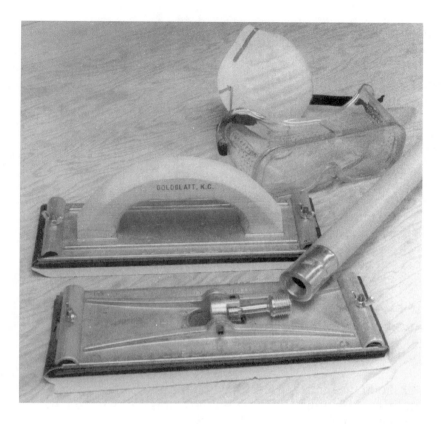

be marred before operators realize it. For drywall sanding, plan to use a combination of hand sanding boards, like these from Stanley Goldblatt. Single units with attached handles are perfect for lower areas; models equipped with swivel connections that attach to long handles make it easy to reach ceilings and tops of walls. Since a lot of sanding dust will be generated, wear goggles and a dust mask.

Belt sanders

The Makita 3-by-21-inch belt sander will remove a great deal of surface material in very little time. A powerful motor drives belts of various grits at high speeds for smooth sanding results with minimal passes. Because this power tool works so well, users must pay strict attention to its operation to avoid sanding too deep. Belts rotate from front to back along the bottom plate, so make sure you have a firm grip before turning it on. Coarse-grit sanding belts combined with the tool's high-torque motor will cause sanders to pull forward quite forcibly.

Sanding belts, like all sandpaper products, are available in different *grits*— varying textures, ranging from very coarse to very smooth. Grits are designated by numbers, lower numbers for the most coarse grits. Since belt sanders are reserved for heavy-duty sanding needs, belt grits generally range only from 40 to 150 grits. For ultrasmooth applications, other types of sandpaper may range to supersmooth 1200 grit.

When starting out on a rough surface, install a 40-grit belt to knock down the roughest parts of the work. Then graduate to a 100-grit belt for better smoothing. Finish the job with a 150-grit belt to achieve maximum smoothness.

All sanding belts are inscribed with an arrow on their inside surface designating the direction the belt is designed to move. The Makita belt sander also features an arrow that indicates the direction of drum rotation. Make sure belts are installed with their arrows matching the tool's to ensure proper performance.

Even though this Makita belt sander is equipped with an impressive built-in dust-collection system that results in most dust being deposited into the bag, some dust will escape to the surrounding atmosphere. Therefore, wear goggles and a dust mask whenever sanding with this tool.

To remove and install sanding belts, first unplug the tool from its power source. Then pull out the locking lever to release tension on the installed belt. Pull off the old belt and slip on a new one. Position belts as close to their proper position as possible before locking them in place by pushing in the locking lever.

Assured that the sanding belt is properly positioned and secured according to operating instructions, you can make final belt adjustments on this belt sander by rotating this knob featured on the tool's left front side. With the tool running, this knob is slowly turned to make the belt move toward the left or right to position the belt in the center of the sander's power drum.

Large belt sanders are often too big for many sanding tasks. For those occasions when a skinny sander is needed for close work, consider the Makita 1⅛-by-21-inch belt sander. Like the bigger sanders, this model requires belts to be installed according to the arrow indicators provided on their interior sides. An arrow on this sander's power drum helps users quickly determine in which direction belts will be driven.

A handle provided with Makita 1⅛-by-21-inch belt sanders can be moved to an upright or down position to accommodate work. It can also be removed for those confined-space sanding jobs. All belt sanders, including smaller models, are designed for rapid sanding. Allowing them to rest in one spot will cause the formation of grooves; therefore, plan to keep belt sanders moving at all times and stop them often to check sanding progress.

Finishing sanders

The Makita random-orbit sander is lightweight, has a palm-grip design for one-handed operation, and utilizes a random-orbit sanding action for supersmooth sanding. It does not spin around in fast circles but moves in numerous back-and-forth, side-to-side eccentric motions.

This model's sanding-disk application utilizes a very simple and easy hook-and-loop system where soft fibers on disk backs grip firmly to sturdy hooks featured on the sander's base, just like Velcro. Disks are available in a variety of grits.

To minimize dust, use an optional Makita dust-collector hose. The small end attaches to a port on the sander; a larger end fits right into the hose of Makita wet-dry vacuum machines. In addition, you must be sure that holes in these sandpaper disks line up with the holes on the sander's base. Sanding dust is picked up through these holes and pulled through sanders and hose into vacuum cleaners. When not using a vacuum, cover the dust port with the rubber cap provided.

For small jobs requiring fine finish results, consider the Makita finishing sander. Models like this are commonly referred to as *palm sanders* because they are small, easy to maneuver, and fit into the palm of your hand.

To take full advantage of this sander's ability to pull sanding dust into its handy collection bag, you must punch holes in sandpaper that match those holes featured on the tool's base. A punch plate is designed with guide lips that make it easy to determine how it is positioned before punching holes in sandpaper that line up with those on the sander's base.

A Makita cordless finishing sander vibrates sandpaper sheets in a back-and-forth movement for fine sanding along wood grains. The power finishing sander with cord operates in much the same way—back-and-forth movements. Its base is bigger than the cordless model and will cover more surface with each pass.

Both sanders offer excellent results. The cordless unit is great for jobs inside cabinets and in other spaces where an electrical cord may get in the way or electrical power is not available, like vacation cabins in rural areas. The larger finishing sander with an electrical cord has a wide base to offer more coverage with each pass.

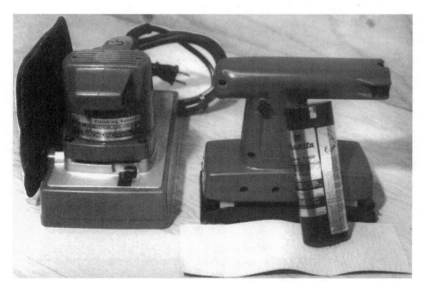

Belt-disk sander

In a workshop or craft room, a stationary belt-disk sander might be perfect for sanding jobs on pieces destined to adorn bookcases, cabinets, decorative shelves, and other items.

This 4-inch belt and 6-inch disk sander from Harbor Freight Tools features an adjustable-belt sander that can be used vertically, horizontally, or at any angle in between. A removable backstop supports your work in either direction. The featured cast-aluminum sanding disk includes a tilting table that locks at any position from 0 degrees to 45 degrees for bevel sanding. Belt-disk sanders must be operated strictly according to directions to avoid mishaps on work and hands and fingers. Wear goggles and a dust mask during sanding activities.

Grinders

Removing slag, rust, and corrosion from metal is best accomplished with a *grinder*. Sturdy grinding wheels are capable of smoothing metal quickly. Be advised that such operations will cause sparks to fly, so make sure all combustible materials are removed from your workplace.

The Makita 5-inch angle grinder can be outfitted with a grinding wheel, heavy-duty coarse-grit sanding disks, or an assortment of wire-brush attachments. Always keep the tool's safety guard accurately positioned during a grinding procedure. Safety goggles, a dust mask, and leather gloves should be worn while grinding, sanding, or cleaning metal with a wire-brush attachment.

Lots of projects will require some type of sanding endeavor. Since sanding is generally the last procedure to finish projects, you may tend to get in a hurry to complete the work to get started staining or painting. Do yourself a favor and plan an adequate time to finish sanding endeavors completely. Minor flaws on wood surfaces will be accentuated once stain or paint has been applied. Surfaces sanded to perfection should result in glassy stain or paint finishes with deep rich lusters.

CHAPTER 10

Maintenance & repair

MAJOR REPAIRS to any power tool or equipment should be made only by qualified factory-trained technicians. Inferior repair work or mistakes in putting parts back together correctly at specified torque calibrations could result in tool failure with parts thrown out from high-speed motors like shrapnel.

On the other hand, routine maintenance and minor repairs covered in operating instructions should be part of an ongoing tool and equipment preventive maintenance program.

Cleaning

Tools used to cut, bore, shape, or smooth wood will get covered with sawdust, sanding dust, or some other type of wood residue. Even the most powerful types of vacuum and dust-control systems cannot pick up 100 percent of all the dust particles created during woodworking. Therefore, plan on spending a few minutes after completing tasks to clean tools, so that they will be ready for work the next time you need them.

A soft, dry floppy paintbrush works great for dislodging and whisking away sawdust and other wood-residue accumulations from tools. Used in conjunction with a household vacuum brush accessory at the end of a powerful vacuum, tools can be cleaned in just minutes.

The Makita 8-gallon wet-dry vacuum has a strong suction capacity and large reservoir for holding a lot of debris. In addition, this unit can pick up water and other nonflammable liquids. Use a shop vacuum like this one for lots of dust-cleaning chores.

Minor service & repair

All circular saws are equipped with a means for locking the power shaft during blade changes. The Makita hypoid saw has

such a button located at the front of its motor housing. With
the tool unplugged, push in the button and slowly rotate the
blade by hand. Once the button's shaft lines up with a
corresponding slot, it will go in toward the motor farther and
lock the power shaft in place. With your finger still on the
button, use the saw's wrench to loosen the bolt that secures the
blade in place. Note: Many such blade-securing bolts on
circular saws are equipped with left-hand threads; this means

that they operate in the opposite direction of normal bolts—clockwise to loosen and counterclockwise to tighten.

Many Makita instruction manuals include information about replacing worn motor *brushes*. These components (two) are spring-loaded to ride against armatures and help make motors turn.

Removal and replacement of most Makita motor brushes is a quick and simple task. On the hypoid saw, for example, just unscrew brush caps (one on each side), pull out old brushes, put in new brushes, and replace caps. That's it. Makita recommends checking brushes regularly and replacing both at the same time as soon as either one is worn down to its wear-limit mark.

Occasionally, a power cord attached to a power tool will become cut or damaged. Since most power-tool work requires use of extension cords, plan to insert a new plug at damaged sections instead of splicing or taping damaged cords together. It is much safer to use a short cord and extension cord than to rely on spliced cords.

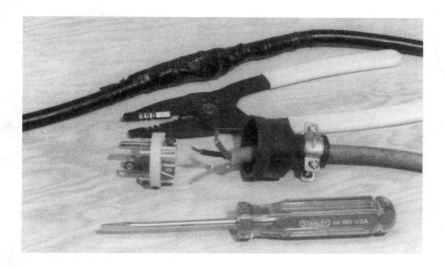

Stanley Jobmaster pliers work great for stripping insulation from wires. Look closely at faces of new plugs for information that shows how far back to strip wires. Appliance cords normally include three colored wires connected to specific terminals inside plugs. The green (ground) wire is secured to a green screw that generally looks different than the other two screws. The white (neutral) wire is connected to the silver terminal, and the black (hot) wire is screwed into the gold- or brass-colored terminal. Inspect plugs closely to note if embossed writing indicates which wire color goes to which terminal.

An all-purpose bench grinder is a handy asset for almost any workshop. Generally, common bench grinders feature a grinding wheel on one side and a heavy-duty wire brush on the other.

A Baldor bench grinder from The Eastwood Company makes quick work of cleaning up an older wood-splitting maul before a new handle is attached. Bench grinders are equipped with clear protective shields that must be adjusted before work begins. Tool rests are provided as a means of controlling workpieces. Always wear safety goggles when working with bench grinders.

Sharpening tools & accessories

Sharpening chisels, planer blades, knives, and other cutting implements can be done by hand on a *sharpening stone*, the process called *honing*.

The Makita sharpening stone carries a recommendation to soak the entire stone in water for two minutes before putting it to use. The reason for soaking is to lubricate the sharpening process. Other types of honing stones may accept light oil applications; be sure to read instructions.

Sharpening by hand for most tool blades requires a *guide*. When operated according to instructions, guides assist users in sharpening items to recommended bevel angles. Tool blades perform best when they are sharpened to those bevels.

The Stanley honing guide works great for hand-plane blades and wood chisels. A plastic flip-out gauge shows users how far out to extend blades or chisel ends for honing procedures to result in preferred bevel angles. Once a blade has been adjusted into the guide correctly, screws in the back are tightened to secure the blade in place. The plastic gauge is snapped back into a locking holder.

Operating the honing guide is easy. It is balanced on top of a sharpening stone by a roller in back and the blade that is being honed in front. To sharpen, place the unit on top of a moistened stone (water or oil, as instructions indicate) and with a reciprocating motion, roll the guide back and forth with a slight downward pressure.

Check the cutting edge to ensure that an even hone angle is being obtained. Continue this operation until the entire hand-plane blade or chisel is sharpened uniformly. Be very careful when removing sharp blades or chisels from the honing guide after sharpening. Their honed ends will be exceptionally sharp.

Power-planer blades can also be sharpened on stones if the process is accomplished with an appropriate guide. A Makita sharpening-holder assembly is available for all Makita power planers. Holders are designed for certain-size blades.

Since Makita planers feature two cutting blades, holder-assembly sets for them are equipped to handle two blades at once. One blade is positioned at the base of the holder, the other at the top. Once blades have been positioned according to directions, they are moved across the sharpening stone to make perfect bevel angles and sharp edges.

Operating the sharpening holder assembly to sharpen power-planer cutting blades must be done exactly as instructions dictate. Securing blades in the unit inaccurately will result in blemished blade edges that may not be easy to remedy. Remember too that each time blades are sharpened, their size becomes shorter as parts of the tip are honed away.

Sharpening circular-saw blades requires a technique much different from those for planer and chisel blades. Although many saw shops may offer inexpensive blade exchanges, you may prefer to keep your blades and have them sharpened. One never knows what kind of abuse another blade has been subjected to or how long the exchanged one will last.

A good alternative to blade exchanges or having someone else sharpen them, is the Makita 5-inch bench grinder. This equipment is especially set up to sharpen circular-saw blades and planer blades. Its blade-sharpening kit includes all of the accessories needed to grind blades accurately to uniform bevel angles. The grinding wheel positioned on the saw-blade-sharpening side of the unit is very slim and has a bevel on the edge for circular-saw blades.

Operating instructions must be studied and followed closely to ensure precise results. Consider having a new blade on hand to compare to help you understand exactly how these blades are supposed to be sharpened.

Once a circular-saw blade has been made perfectly round, the sharpening tool rest must be adjusted to a 15-degree angle. Help from a protractor is useful. The tool rest is adjusted to 15 degrees on one side for sharpening half (every other tooth) of the teeth and then positioned to 15 degrees on the other side for the other half (every other tooth). Expect to spend some time practicing with this tool before becoming expert.

Adjustable eyeshields are provided for the Makita bench grinder, and you must use them each time the tool is operated. In addition, since you will be grinding metal, plan to wear safety goggles and a dust mask.

Sharpening planer blades on the Makita bench grinder is very easy. Secured in their proper holder assembly, blades are moved across the specially beveled grinding wheel to make sharp bevel angles. A screw mechanism operates the sharpening tool rest in a precise and controlled manner.

Because no lubrication is available for blade sharpening, plan to sharpen planer blades slowly, a little at a time. Abrasive wheels grinding on metal will create sparks, and you can bet metal blades will get hot. Blade damage can occur if the blade is exposed to too much concentrated heat.

Many home-improvement projects will flow more smoothly and be completed more quickly when tools and equipment operate as expected on the first try. Having to stop projects soon after starting to replace dull blades or clean wood residue from indicator marks will be unnecessary if you clean and service tools after each use. While cleaning, always take an extra moment or two making sure screws, nuts, bolts, levers, and adjustable accessories are tight. Don't forget to wash goggles with mild detergent and water.

Tool & equipment extras

HUNDREDS of other tools and accessories may make a lot of home-improvement endeavors a little less strenuous or inexpensive to accomplish.

This chapter offers a brief look at some specialty tools, workshop and equipment accessories, and remodeling products.

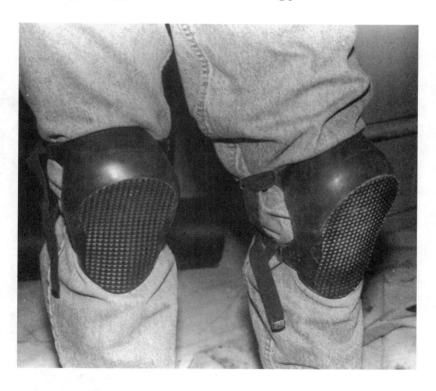

Heavy-duty knee pads from Stanley Goldblatt are worth their weight in gold when working on floors, decks, and other projects requiring long periods of kneeling.

Screwing down subfloor material, cutting and stapling building paper, and installing baseboard moldings are perfect examples of where quality knee pads would be greatly appreciated.

Every remodeling job will result in dirty and dusty conditions. A powerful Makita 8-gallon wet-dry vacuum with large storage capacity makes quick work of most cleanup chores. The wand attachment is equipped with a removable brush for dry work and a removable *squeegee* for wet jobs. A wheeled base on this vacuum makes it very easy to maneuver around rooms to accomplish lots of vacuum work in little time. The nozzle attachments from your household vacuum cleaner should also fit on the Makita vacuum hose. Use a brush for cleaning tools and the crevice tool for reaching into tight spaces.

The Makita 10-inch table saw cuts through wood with precision. The amount of sawdust it creates is incredible. To reduce sawdust accumulations, consider setting up a Makita dust collector. For Makita's dust collector to work properly on the table saw, a piece of plywood must be cut to cover the opening in the table-saw stand. Simply remove the saw from its stand, measure the bottom of the saw base, and cut a piece of plywood to fit. Mark the locations for mounting bolts and drill ⅜-inch holes at each spot.

Once the plywood piece has been drilled, put it on the stand and replace the saw. Tighten mounting bolts securely. Then retrieve the optional table-saw hood and attach it per instructions to the bottom of the base just above the stand. The high cubic feet per minute (CFM) ability of the Makita dust-collector vacuum unit will pull out almost all sawdust between the table saw and the piece of plywood.

Notice that there is almost no sawdust on the floor, even after making six cuts through these boards. Sawdust is pulled through the blade opening and into the enclosed space between it and the plywood by suction provided by the dust collector. A large corrugated hose attached to the hood routes sawdust directly into the storage bag. The bag has a large clear window that allows users to see when it needs to be emptied.

The same dust collector can be hooked up to the Makita planer-jointer providing optional hoods have been installed on those pieces of equipment.

Along with keeping sawdust and wood shavings to a minimum in your workshop, this system will provide you with clean wood sawdust and shavings that can be placed in flower beds and other decorative landscape surroundings. With the Makita dust collector hose moved to the storage-bag port and a special fitting placed over the intake port, a *blower nozzle* can be used for blowing dust off tools and equipment. The blower nozzle works well for dusting off workbench tops, cabinet-door edges, nooks and crannies along floor edges, and a host of other things.

When you purchase a brand-new Campbell Hausfeld 5-HP air compressor, plan to spend adequate time setting it up. Along with putting oil into the motor, an experienced electrician will have to hook up the 220-volt power supply. This is a heavy-voltage wiring job that must be taken very seriously. A compressed-air outlet port is featured on the side of this tank. Per directions, install proper fittings that will couple with your air-supply hose.

The hand-carried 1-HP portable air compressor from Campbell Hausfeld is easy to move about and provides plenty of compressed air for pneumatic staplers and nailers. Brand new, this unit requires the installation of an air-hose coupling. Units do not come with couplings because it is impossible to determine which type or style of couplings customers need. This small air compressor works off 110-volt household electricity. Plan to use it for any number of projects, inside and outdoors. It is quiet and efficient. When indoors, consider putting the unit on top of a rug, large cloth, or sheet of plywood; vibration could scratch floors.

Shown at the top of the next page is a handy storage box from the Plano Molding Company. Plano manufactures a wide variety of heavy-duty storage containers for all sorts of applications. Their catalog is chock-full of toolboxes, nut and bolt containers, and so on. The drawers on this unit have individual trays that can be sectioned out with plastic dividers. This drawer is filled with Stanley cabinet hinges, door pulls, magnetic catches, and enough screws for all of them.

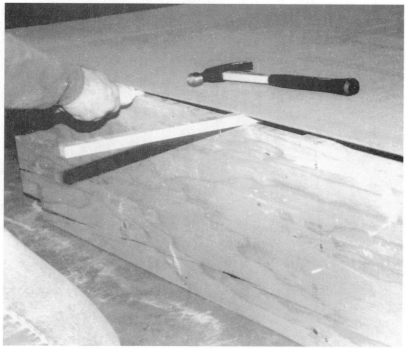

Almost every finish-carpentry task should be accompanied by a quality glue product. Wood glue works exceptionally well to hold pieces of wood together on cabinet faces and backs, and lots of other applications. Plan to nail or screw pieces together too. Blocks of wood hold up a hardboard backing while glue is spread along the plywood edge. Once glue is applied, the blocks will be pulled and the hardboard back nailed into place. Glue will help to keep hardboard firmly affixed. See page 129.

The Makita *heat gun* has a temperature range from 250 degrees to 1,100 degrees F. It will help to strip paint and varnish, loosen tile and putty, thaw frozen metal pipes, remelt adhesives, and perform lots of other tasks that require heat. Be aware that the metal tip will get extremely hot. You must use caution when maneuvering the tool and putting the unit down after completing a job.

Many bathroom and kitchen remodeling jobs will entail some tile work. Plan to use a heavy-duty tile cutter from Harbor Freight Tools. This tool's operation is simple and accurate.

Harbor Freight Tools

Even though a sufficient number of cordless tools may be enough to assist you in constructing an outbuilding on acreage or a cabin in the mountains, you will need a power supply to recharge batteries. For activities that will take place away from normal electrical power supplies, you need a Makita *generator*.

Such a piece of equipment would also be much appreciated during stormy weather when power goes out. A certified electrician must be employed to wire your home's electrical system correctly and safely to accept power from a generator.

Like most all new engines, this Makita generator requires oil in its crankcase before it can be started. A large *warning* tag is affixed to the unit to alert users of this requirement. Read, understand, and follow all operating instructions before starting up and using your Makita generator.

The male electrical plugs used on this machine must have the same ampere (amps) rating as the female outlets. This is an important consideration, since it relates to an incredible amount of electricity. Should too many amps from an outlet be pushed through a male plug that does not have the capacity to handle it, the inferior male plug could get hot enough to catch fire. All endeavors surrounding electricity must be approached with the utmost caution, common sense, and strict adherence to installation instructions and national electrical codes.

Some of the electrical outlets on this generator are equipped with *locking plugs*. Male plugs of the same style are the only ones that will fit and lock into these outlets. Locking electrical plugs are used to ensure cords do not vibrate out of the outlets. Different amp ratings will call for certain plugs. Look at the face of electrical plugs for printing that lists their amp rating. The regular three-prong outlet is a ground fault circuit interrupter.

Wrought-iron railings, fences, gates, and numerous other metal applications will be well served by this HTP America MIG 140 wire-feed welder. It operates off 110-volt current. A bottle of inert welding gas must be used with it to supply an appropriate atmosphere at the nozzle tip for the welding wire; this wire has no flux and must be used with the appropriate inert gas. Operating instructions with this unit are explicit. In addition, HTP America offers a training video program that explains the operation of this welder completely. You are encouraged to acquire the video.

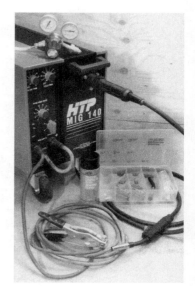

Sheets of drywall are 4 feet wide and from 8 feet to 12 feet long. Drywall is heavy and awkward to carry unless you have a set of *wallboard carriers* from Stanley Goldblatt. These handy tools make carrying drywall and sheets of plywood a snap for two people. One carrier is used at each end of a sheet of drywall or plywood. Gravity and the rubber sleeves prevent sheets from coming loose.

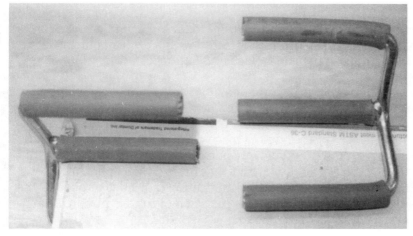

Cutting circles in drywall is easy with the *circle cutter*. Can lights and other round ceiling or wall-mounted amenity locations need to be measured and those measurements transferred to the drywall sheet. Find and mark the center point, determine the radius, and adjust the sliding center pin to fit that radius. Depress and hold the center pin in place, then just work the rolling blade around for a clean cut.

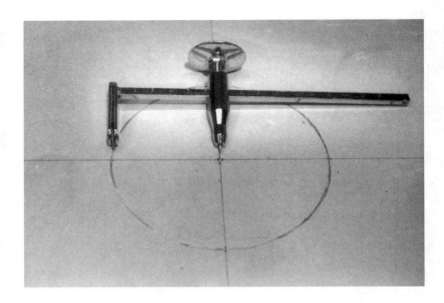

Drywall can be cut with a utility razor knife, circle cutter, or Makita cordless trimmer outfitted with a drywall cutting bit. Remember to measure twice and cut once.

After drywall has been nailed or screwed in place, joints and interior corners must be covered with drywall "mud" and tape; nails or screws are generally covered with just mud. Outside corners are covered with a piece of *corner bead* made of metal, then coated with mud. Only one strip of paper is applied with the initial coat of mud. After that dries, rough spots are knocked down and a wider application of mud is applied. Once it is dry, a third and wider application of mud is put on. That layer will be sanded smooth.

Drywall mud is applied with *drywall knives*. Like big putty knives, these tools do a good job as long as you pay attention to what you are doing. Sizes range from just a few inches wide to a full foot. The Initial mud coat is put on with a 6-inch-wide knife; the second with an 8-inch or 10-inch; the third with a 12-inch. The long-handled model works well for upper walls and ceilings.

To place and smooth drywall mud in corners, use Stanley Goldblatt drywall corner taping tools. On the left is an inside-corner taping tool; on the right is an outside-corner taping tool. As you can see, these tools will make it easy to smooth mud in and on corners.

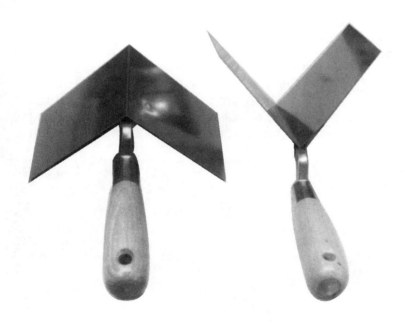

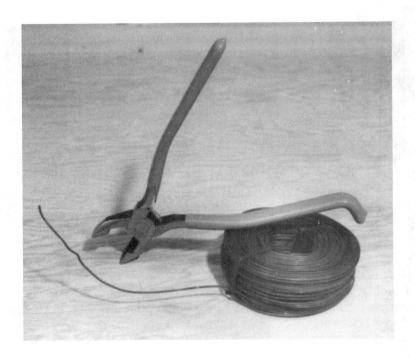

Concrete footings, foundations, walls, and other large projects require pieces of *rebar* to be placed inside forms before concrete is poured. In addition, block walls and chimneys require rebar reinforcement. To keep intersecting pieces of rebar secured together, pieces of *tie wire* are used. This easily bent wire is simple to wrap and secure around rebar with this *ironworker's pliers* tool. Cutters on the tool quickly cut through wire, and the beveled nose pieces are used to twist wire tight against rebar.

Once concrete has been poured, flattened out (*screeded*), and tamped (rocks pushed down), it must be smoothed. The Stanley Goldblatt magnesium float and round-edged Fresno trowel shown on previous page used with extension poles allow finishers to smooth concrete from outside the forms. The magnesium (mag) float is used first since it is heavy and will help to flatten marks made by a tamper. As concrete begins to set up (harden), a Fresno is used much like a steel hand trowel to make the surface smoother and smoother.

A wooden hand float works great while initially pouring concrete to help push or pull concrete into position. This tool also works well for preliminary and early smoothing tasks.

Look at most any sidewalk or driveway and you will notice that the top outside edges are rounded off. This is accomplished with *edgers*. These tools are manufactured with a rounded edge that maneuver over wet concrete to round edges. They are available in different arcs, from a tight ¼-inch to a wide ½-inch; the ones featured here are ⅜-inch. The edger on the left is long and wide and set up with a fitting that attaches to extension poles. It is called a *walking edger* because operators can simply walk along concrete perimeters to round edges. The model on the right with an attached handle is called a *hand edger*.

Again looking at sidewalks and driveways, note the long smooth grooves in them. These are called *control joints* or *seams*. Their purpose is to confine cracks to their length and prevent them from going elsewhere. Used in conjunction with expansion joints, seams help to confine concrete cracks.

Seams are made initially in wet concrete and then smoothed over and over again with *seamers*. The machined protrusion extending from seamer bases causes rocks and concrete material to be pushed down and away, leaving behind a smooth groove. The tool on the left is a *walking seamer*; the one on the right is a *hand seamer*.

Designed somewhat like drywall corner taping tools, concrete step trowels are used to finish inside and outside step corners. See photo at the top of next page. The upper portion of the photo shows an *outside-corner step-finishing trowel*; the bottom portion shows an *inside-corner step finishing trowel*.

Once concrete has set up with a rather hard surface, *steel finishing trowels* are used to bring that surface to smooth perfection. An assortment of sizes and styles are available. The trowels with rounded ends may be best for beginning concrete finishers since they do not leave surface ridges nearly as pronounced as the squared-off models. On the far left is a

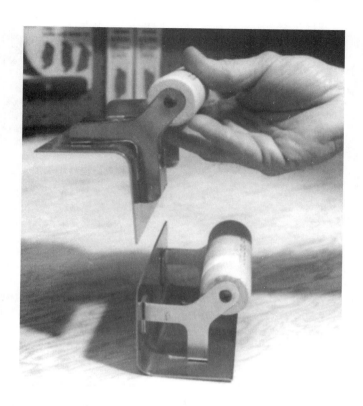

magnesium hand float. Like the wood hand float, this tool is used for initial concrete placement and smoothing.

When concrete has become hard enough to support steel-trowel finishing, workers have to get out in the middle of slabs to finish those areas. For years, many professional and do-it-yourself concrete finishers have used small pieces of plywood

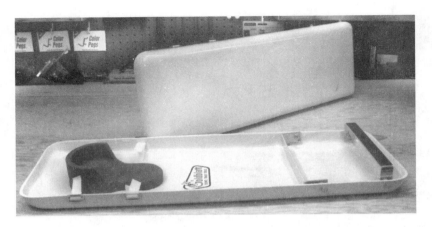

as platforms to support them. Using two, they leapfrog around finishing off the marks made by plywood as they go. With these *concrete kneeboards* from Stanley Goldblatt, finishers will have a lot less work to do troweling out such marks. In addition, they can enjoy the comfort of built-in kneepads.

Really smooth concrete is as slick as ice when wet. This is why most people prefer a broom finish to their outdoor walkways, patios, driveways, and other slabs. By simply drawing a soft broom across freshly finished concrete, hundreds of tiny lines will offer a great deal of traction and stability when concrete gets wet.

Occasionally, especially during major remodeling projects, old concrete has to be cut out. For major cutting operations, seek the help of a professional concrete-cutting company. Large jobs require special tools and equipment.

On the other hand, for smaller cutting jobs, like taking out a short section of foundation for the installation of a sliding glass door, consider the use of a Makita dry diamond concrete cutting blade attached to the Makita 5-inch angle grinder. This blade is designed to cut concrete, tile, brick, stone, and similar materials. (This grinder's safety guard is hidden behind the diamond blade. Use safety guards for all applications and be certain they are positioned for maximum protection, per operating instructions.)

Patio, carport, and other outdoor coverings supported by posts include a means to keep those posts from being knocked out of position at their base. More than likely, these posts are supported by a *post anchor*. These items are designed to have their supporting rod placed in wet concrete, while the base rests just a little above the concrete surface. They are installed this way to help keep water from coming in contact with wood posts. A number of other styles are available through the Simpson Strong-Tie Connector Company.

A huge selection of connectors are designed to join lumber for all sorts of construction needs from gazebos to decks, mudsills, and top plates. Every metal connector you will ever need can be found in the Simpson Strong-Tie Connector catalog. In addition to construction connectors, Simpson offers a variety of products designed for workbenches, log holders, and storage-shelf units. Making use of these handy connectors could save you a lot of time.

When planning a room addition or home remodel, it is very difficult at times to visualize exactly what the rooms or structure will look like when completed. This is a common dilemma experienced by thousands of do-it-yourselfers. To help you get a much better idea of what you want to build and how different home appliances and furnishings will fit in the dimensions of your project, consider the Autodesk Retail Products home series computer programs.

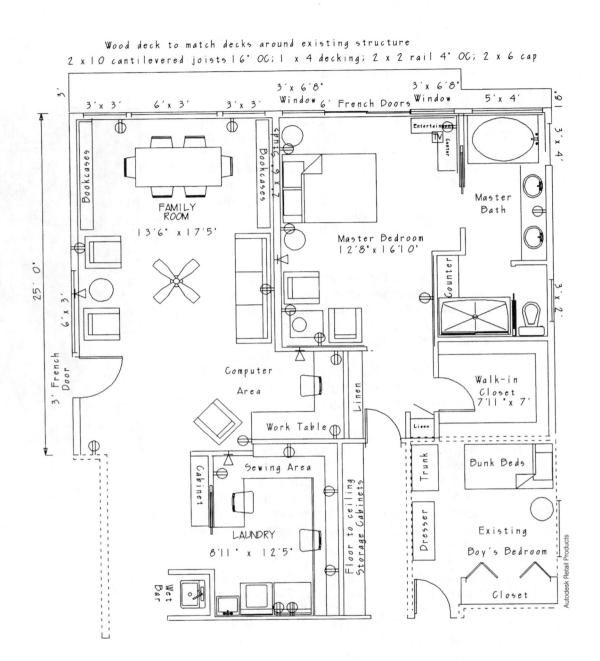

Wood deck to match decks around existing structure
2 x 10 cantilevered joists 16" OC; 1 x 4 decking; 2 x 2 rail 4" OC; 2 x 6 cap

Autodesk Retail Products

Used with appropriate computer hardware, this series of programs can help you understand what you want to build or remodel. In addition to the home program displayed here, there are programs for bathrooms and decks. Autodesk also offers a 3-D program that allows users to see their planned addition or remodel in three dimensions. Although originally designed to help homeowners express their building or remodeling ideas to professional architects, many users have become so well acquainted with these programs that they draw up their own sets of building plans and have them accepted by municipal building departments.

Almost every home-improvement project will require some kind of ladder, and Keller Ladders offers any style needed. Working on ladders can be dangerous when you maneuver in awkward positions or fail to set up ladders in their recommended positions. When using a *wood step ladder*, make sure it is located where you can reach work areas with comfort and stability.

Setting up *extension ladders* safely and efficiently mandates careful attention to positioning. According to Keller Ladders, the proper climbing angle for extension ladders is 75½ degrees. To achieve that angle, place the ladder base one-fourth of the working length from the support or wall. *Working length* is the distance along the side rails from the bottom of the ladder to the support points. (The ladder base should be placed a minimum of 3 feet from the vertical support.) To gain access to roofs, ladder tops should extend at least 3 feet above the point of support at eaves, gutter, or roofline.

Hanging drywall is labor-intensive work; sheets are heavy and cumbersome. Covering ceilings with drywall by one person is virtually impossible; that is, unless that person is using a PanelLift drywall lift from Telpro. See page 144. This machine is simple to set up, can be easily and quickly dismantled for storage in areas no bigger than many full-size automobile trunks, and makes hanging drywall a job that one person can accomplish, even on ceilings. If you are planning a large-scale project, consider a PanelLift drywall lift.

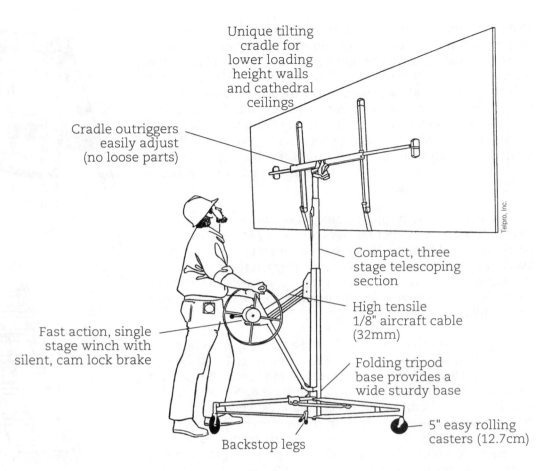

Unique tilting cradle for lower loading height walls and cathedral ceilings

Cradle outriggers easily adjust (no loose parts)

Compact, three stage telescoping section

High tensile 1/8" aircraft cable (32mm)

Fast action, single stage winch with silent, cam lock brake

Folding tripod base provides a wide sturdy base

5" easy rolling casters (12.7cm)

Backstop legs

Telpro, Inc.

Home-improvement endeavors will almost always call for paint work. To make those tasks much easier and quicker, employ the HousePainter from Campbell Hausfeld. This airless paint sprayer can apply latex, water, and oil paints, stains, and sealers. It takes only five minutes to set up the machine, and the high-pressure hose measures 25 feet. Airless spray painters do an excellent job of applying paint with minimal overspray. The best time to use them is when weather is nice and breezes are minimal or nonexistent.

It is always nice to have tools close at hand when they are needed. This is especially true when working on roofs, ladders, or other places where it may be quite inconvenient to stop what you are doing and walk to where tools, nails, or other desired implements are sitting. Therefore, invest in a quality *tool belt* like this one from Alta Industries. In addition to tool belts, kneepads, and other work accessories, Alta Industries offers handy holsters for cordless tools.

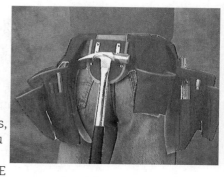

Eagle windows are available in numerous styles and shapes, and the quality of their construction is second to none. You may order Eagle Maximizer Low-E gas-filled dual-sealed insulated glass for any Eagle product. In the summer, Low-E coating cuts radiant heat flow to the inside. In the winter, it reduces flow to the outside. The gas filling boosts the insulation value (R-4) to about double that of ordinary glass (R-2). In addition, the Maximizer blocks harmful ultraviolet rays by as much as 70 percent without reducing light or visibility, protecting furniture, draperies, photos, and other furnishings and adornments.

Without a doubt, beautiful and efficient windows can turn an ordinary house into a beautiful, warm, and comfortable home. Before ripping off siding and cutting new window holes in solid walls, spend time with your local Eagle window and door representative to learn exactly how their windows are installed for new and remodeling projects. Manufacturing is so precise and tolerances so close with these quality windows that rough openings are made tighter for these than for many other brands of windows and doors.

When I first started working on this book, my family knew I had a soft spot in my heart for all kinds of tools and equipment. They would find me in the garage or workshop for hours, cleaning, sorting, and just having a good time puttering. Once I started displaying the fruits of my (and the tools') labors, they were amazed at what the tools and equipment in this book could do.

I guess they had thought that quality furnishings and accessories were made by Santa's elves. You should have seen the size of their eyes when I told them that they could be taught to make the same things with a little time, patience, complete attention to operating and safety instructions, and guidance from the guru of how-to.

This book is filled with lots of efficient tools, pieces of equipment, and accessories. All are capable of completing the jobs they were designed to do. The only element that manufacturers have no control over is operator error. Again and again throughout this book you have been advised to follow manufacturers' recommendations as they are printed in operating instructions. You have also been advised to wear safety goggles and dust masks for dust, debris, flying particles, and other objects.

It is my sincere hope you will be completely successful in your home-improvement endeavors and that the jobs you undertake to make your home more beautiful and efficient are accomplished safely and efficiently on the first try.

Sources

As an active do-it-yourselfer, you are encouraged to contact the following companies by telephone or letter to request catalogs and other information about their tools, equipment, or home-improvement products.

Alta Industries
PO Box 2764
Santa Rosa, CA 95405
(800) 248-5633
tool belts

American Plywood Association
7011 South 19th Street
Tacoma, WA 98411
(206) 565-6600
information and plans

American Tool Companies, Inc.
PO Box 337
Dewitt, NE 68341
(402) 683-2315
Quick-Vise-Grips, and more

Autodesk Retail Products
1911 North Creek Parkway South
Bothell, WA 98011
(800) 228-3601
computer plan-making software

Behr Process Corporation
3400 W. Segerstrom Avenue
Santa Ana, CA 92704
(800) 854-0133
paints, stains, and varnishes

Campbell Hausfeld
100 Production Drive
Harrison, OH 45030
(513) 367-4811
air compressors and pneumatic tools

Cedar Shake and Shingle Bureau
515 116th Avenue NE, Suite 275
Bellevue, WA 98004-5294
(206) 453-1323
information

Dupont Tyvek
Wilmington, DE 19880-0722
(800) 44-Tyvek
house wrap

DAP, Inc.
PO Box 277
Dayton, OH 45401
(800) 568-4554
caulk, glue, paint, etc.

Eagle Windows and Doors
375 East Ninth Street
PO Box 1072
Dubuque, IA 52004-1072
(319) 556-2270
high-quality windows and doors

The Eastwood Company
580 Lancaster Avenue, Box 296
Malvern, Pa 19355
(800) 345-1178
tools for working with metal

Empire Brushes, Inc.
PO Box 1606
Greenville, NC 27835-1606
(919) 758-4111
brushes and brooms

Freud
PO Box 7187
High Point, NC 27264
(800) 472-7307
biscuit cutters and more

General Cable Co.
4 Tesseneer Drive
Highland Heights, KY 41076
(606) 572-8000
Fax: (606) 572-9634
Romex® cable

Harbor Freight Tools
Central Purchasing, Inc.
3491 Mission Oaks Boulevard
Camarillo, CA 93011-3169
(800) 423-2567
large variety of tools and equipment

HTP America
261 Woodwork Lane
Palatine, IL 60067
(800) 872-9353
welders and metal cutters

Keller Ladder Company
18000 State Road Nine
Miami, FL 33162
(800) 222-2600
ladders and ladder accessories

Leslie-Locke, Inc.
4501 Circle 75 Parkway, Suite F-6300
Atlanta, GA 30339
skylights and roof windows

Levition Manufacturing Company, Inc.
59-25 Little Neck Parkway
Little Neck, NY 11362-2591
(718) 229-4040
electrical outlets and switches

McGuire-Nicholas Company, Inc.
2331 Tubeway Avenue
City of Commerce, CA 90040
(213) 722-6961
tool belts

Makita U.S.A., Inc.
14930 Northam Street
La Mirada, CA 90638-5753
(714) 522-8088
cordless/power tools and equipment

NuTone
Madison and Red Bank Roads
Cincinnati, OH 45227-1599
(800) 543-8687
built-in convenience products

PanelLift Telpro, Inc.
Route 1, Box 138
Grand Forks, ND 58201
(800) 441-0551
drywall/wallboard lift

Plano Molding Company
431 East South Street
Plano, IL 60545-1601
(708) 552-3111
toolboxes and storage containers

Plumb Shop (Brass-Craft)
100 Galleria Officentre
Southfield, MI 48034
(313) 827-1100
plumbing parts and accessories

Power Products Company
Cayuga and Ramena Streets
Philadelphia, PA 19120
(800) 346-7833
fluorescent lights

Simpson Strong-Tie Connector Company, Inc.
1450 Doolittle Drive
San Leandro, CA 94577
(800) 999-5099
metal connectors

The Stanley Works
1000 Stanley Drive
New Britain, CT 06053
(203) 225-5111
hand tools, hardware, and accessories

STA-PUT, Inc.
23504 29th Avenue West
Lynnwood, WA 98036-8318
locking pegboard hooks in different styles

Structron Corporation
1980 Diamond Street
San Marcos, CA 92069
(619) 744-6371
shovels and outdoor tools

Weiser Lock
6660 S. Broadmoor Road
Tucson, AZ 85746
(800) 488- LOCK
door knobs, handles, and locks

Western Wood Products Association
Yeon Building
522 SW Fifth Avenue
Portland, OR 97204-2122
(503) 224-3930
information and plans

Zircon Corporation
1580 Dell Avenue
Campbell, CA 95008
(800) 245-9265
water level

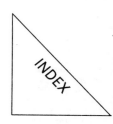

The NailingGluingLevelingHoldingPullingClamping Tool.

QUICK-GRIP® Bar Clamps.
Available wherever quality tools are sold.

 **QUICK·GRIP®**
A UNIT OF **AMERICAN TOOL** COMPANIES, INC.

 CAMPBELL HAUSFELD ★ **PROFESSIONAL**

- Air compressors
- Air tools
- Accessories

- Paint sprayers
- Pneumatic nailers
- Fasteners

CALL 1-800-543-8622
for a free brochure

Let EAGLE® complement your great ideas with energy-efficient windows and doors in a universe of shapes, sizes and colors. For more information and to receive your free brochure, please complete and send in the attached coupon.

Please send me free literature on your products.

I plan to: ☐ build ☐ remodel ☐ replace
☐ immediately ☐ within the next 3-6 months
☐ within the next 6-12 months

Name_____
Address_____
City_____ State_____
Zip_____ Phone_____

Send to
EAGLE Window and Door, Inc.
P.O. Box 1072
Dubuque, IA 52004-1072

EAGLE WINDOWS · DOORS
A MASCO COMPANY

DJ-MH

COUPON #112-031-099

CALL 1-800-423-2567 FOR YOUR
FREE!
HARBOR FREIGHT TOOLS CATALOG NOW!

PROFESSIONAL & DO-IT-YOURSELFER TOOLS

HARBOR FREIGHT TOOLS
$5.00 OFF COUPON*
CHARGE IT! 1-800-423-2567
DISCOVER/NOVUS VISA MasterCard AMERICAN EXPRESS

*THIS COUPON IS VALID FOR ONE ORDER OF $15.00 OR MORE. ONE COUPON PER CUSTOMER.

157